Homework

Other titles in the Resource Books for Teachers series

Beginners
Peter Grundy

Classroom Dynamics
Jill Hadfield

Conversation
Rob Nolasco and Lois Arthur

Cultural Awareness
Barry Tomalin and Susan Stempleski

Dictionaries
Jon Wright

Drama
Charlyn Wessels

Exam Classes
Peter May

Film
Susan Stempleski and Barry Tomalin

Grammar Dictation
Ruth Wajnryb

The Internet
Scott Windeatt, David Hardisty, and David Eastment

Learner-based Teaching
Colin Campbell and Hanna Kryszewska

Listening
Goodith White

Literature
Alan Maley and Alan Duff

Music and Song
Tim Murphey

Newspapers
Peter Grundy

Project Work 2nd edition
Diana L. Fried-Booth

Pronunciation
Clement Laroy

Role Play
Gillian Porter Ladousse

Vocabulary 2nd edition
John Morgan and Mario Rinvolucri

Writing
Tricia Hedge

Primary Resource Books

Art and Crafts with Children
Andrew Wright

Assessing Young Learners
Sophie Ioannou-Georgiou and Pavlos Pavlou

Creating Stories with Children
Andrew Wright

Drama with Children
Sarah Phillips

Games for Children
Gordon Lewis with Günther Bedson

The Internet and Young Learners
Gordon Lewis

Projects with Young Learners
Diane Phillips, Sarah Burwood, and Helen Dunford

Storytelling with Children
Andrew Wright

Very Young Learners
Vanessa Reilly and Sheila M. Ward

Writing with Children
Jackie Reilly and Vanessa Reilly

Young Learners
Sarah Phillips

Resource Books for Teachers
series editor Alan Maley

Homework

Lesley Painter

OXFORD
UNIVERSITY PRESS

Great Clarendon Street, Oxford OX2 6DP

Oxford University Press is a department of the University of Oxford.
It furthers the University's objective of excellence in research, scholarship,
and education by publishing worldwide in

Oxford New York

Auckland Bangkok Buenos Aires Cape Town Chennai
Dar es Salaam Delhi Hong Kong Istanbul Karachi Kolkata
Kuala Lumpur Madrid Melbourne Mexico City Mumbai Nairobi
São Paulo Shanghai Singapore Taipei Tokyo Toronto

OXFORD and OXFORD ENGLISH are registered trade marks of
Oxford University Press in the UK and in certain other countries

First published 2003

ISBN 0 19 437574 9

Printed in China

Acknowledgements

The authors and publisher are grateful to those who have given permission to reproduce the following extracts and adaptations of copyright material:

'Homework code' from *New Headway* by Liz and John Soars © Oxford University Press 1986. Reproduced by permission.

'Vietnam's vanishing primates' by Connie Rogers, *The New York Times*, 28 July 2002. Reproduced by permission of The New York Times.

'Mary, 88, shows the way behind the bar' by Adele Edmondson, *Shropshire Star*, 29 April 2002 and 'Mystery as postcard arrives 80 years late', *Shropshire Star*, 7 March 1998. Reproduced by permission of Shropshire Star.

Although every effort has been made to trace and contact copyright holders before publication, this has not been possible in some cases. We apologize for any apparent infringement of copyright and, if notified, the publisher will be pleased to rectify any errors or omissions at the earliest opportunity.

Line drawings by Ann Johns.

The publisher would like to thank the following for permission to use photographs:

Photos on page 58 supplied by Oxford University Press

Contents

The author and series editor	1
Foreword	3
Introduction	5
What is homework?	5
The role of homework	5
Re-evaluating homework	6
A new approach	8
In conclusion	11
How each activity is organized	12

		Time (in minutes) in class	homework	Aims	Page
1	**Getting started**				13
	Working homework into your curriculum				13
	Memory work				14
	Dictionary skills				14
	Monitoring homework and providing feedback				15
1.1	**My homework book**			To make homework exercises as important as class tasks and for students to identify the aims behind homework tasks	16
1.2	**Correcting homework**			To encourage students to correct their own errors and to identify their own areas of weakness	16
1.3	**Comments to add to homework**			To add fun to the comments you write on homework, and to create a fun dialogue with your students	17
1.4	**Sending homework home in an envelope**			To set homework in a different way, which will motivate students to do the work	18
1.5	**Mission impossible**	15		To add variety to the way that homework is set	18
1.6	**Send a word via email**	15		To deliver homework via email	19

		Time (in minutes) in class	homework	Aims	Page
2	**Focus on homework**				20
2.1	Setting up homework	20–30	30–40	To allow students to provide feedback on homework tasks, and say what they found useful and effective.	21
2.2	My favourite task	10–15	30–40	To motivate the students by doing activities they enjoy. Students will begin to feel confident making their own decisions about how to learn, rather than relying on the teacher for constant guidance	27
2.3	Design a homework task for your group	10–15	30–60	To give the students the responsibility of creating a homework task for their class	28
2.4	Skills work	10–15	40+	To allow students to bring activities to class that they find motivating and useful	31
2.5	Letter to the new learners	15–20	30–40	To encourage students to analyse their success as language learners and to consider what helps them best when studying	32
2.6	Teach someone	15–20	60–90	To help students to learn through teaching others.	33
2.7	Homework excuses	45–50	30–40	To show the students that the teacher knows all of the homework excuses already!	35
3	**Focus on lexis**				36
	Usage				36
	Finding examples				37
	The news				37
	Memory				37
3.1	Use it!	10–15	40+	To ensure that students use language from the class and gain confidence speaking in English	39
3.2	Find examples of ...	10–15	40+	To expose students outside class to lexical items taught in class	40
3.3	Words from the news	20–30	30–40	To expose students to lexical items which are currently in use in world English, while also making the language of the news more familiar to them	41
3.4	English bag	15–20	15–20	To create an effective way of storing new vocabulary items which is accessible, portable, and convenient for the students	42
3.5	Word review		50+	To have fun reviewing lexical items while also concentrating on how the words are spelt	44
3.6	Word box	10	40+	To heighten students' awareness of spelling and to allow them to have fun with words	45

		Time (in minutes) in class	homework	Aims	Page
3.7	Finding examples of collocations	10–15	60+	To increase students' exposure to collocations and to make them consider collocations in context	45
3.8	Looking at advertisements	30 +	30–40	To expose the students to language used in advertisements, and to help students feel confident when faced with authentic materials	47
3.9	Collect false friends	15	60+	To make students aware of false friends and to help them to avoid the pitfalls they pose	48
3.10	Match the expression with the day	15–20	50+	To review set expressions that are used on certain occasions in various cultures; to provide an opportunity for students to find out about other cultures and to express information about their own	48
3.11	Body language	10–15	30–40	To present students with thematically related idioms. To make these expressions memorable by using visual aids	50
3.12	Doubles	10–15	40+	To make students aware of this particular type of lexical item and to introduce them to an interesting aspect of English	51
3.13	Oxymorons	15+	60+	To present oxymorons to students, to add interesting lexical items to the students' vocabulary, and to motivate the students with interesting words and expressions	53
3.14	Palindromes	10+	60+	To have fun with lexical items, and also to focus on spelling	54
3.15	Crosswords	20	60+	To ensure that the students go over lexical items at home in terms of spelling and meaning. Crosswords are universal and many students enjoy them in their first language	55
4	**Focus on writing**				**57**
4.1	Diary	15–20	60–90+	To encourage students to write a diary in English in their free time	58
4.2	Letter in a capsule	20–30	50+	To encourage students to write letters in English, developing their letter-writing skills especially as to letter format	60
4.3	Exchanging letters		50+	To encourage students to write letters in English, using a framework	62
4.4	Most romantic love letter	15	40+	To encourage students to write in a fun genre	63
4.5	Expand the story	10	35+	To help students to expand notes into prose; in turn, this should help students to take notes efficiently	65

	Time (in minutes) in class	homework	Aims	Page
4.6 Most unusual facts from the day	15–20+	50–60+	To encourage students to read outside class, and to practise note-taking skills	**66**
4.7 This was the day that …	10–15	40–50	To encourage students to research and present information	**66**
4.8 Scrapbook	20–25	45–50	To encourage students to write, read, speak, and listen to detailed information	**67**
4.9 My photograph	20	40–60	To provide the students with a stimulating personal prompt	**68**
4.10 Pass the story	20–25	20	To make story writing a collaborative experience; the result is a story created jointly, with plenty of anticipation and fun	**69**
4.11 Creative questions	10	30+	To focus students' writing and to personalize their work by using the students' names in the stories	**70**
4.12 Something you would write on a public wall	10–15	40+	To use a fun aspect of writing which is familiar in all cultures. It allows the students to be especially creative with the English language	**71**
4.13 Pocket stories	15–20	30–4	To help students write a story using prompts	**71**

5 Focus on language

5.1 Find examples of …	10–15	40+	To encourage students to search outside class for target language that has been taught	**72**
5.2 Make your own gap-fill	15–20	40+	To vary the usual grammar book/workbook activities by giving students the responsibility of creating their own worksheets	**73**
5.3 Truths about my class	20+	40+	To encourage the students to share information that they know about each other using class-taught language	**75**
5.4 Rhyming simple past	5–10	30+	To revise simple past irregular verbs	**75**
5.5 Colour the text	15	10–15	To review various tenses in a memorable way. This may help students who find visual techniques effective when learning	**76**
5.6 Let's experiment	10–15	60	To encourage students to use the target language outside class	**77**
5.7 What did you hear?	10–15	30+	To encourage grammar practice while using a much-loved medium—television—as the prompt	**79**
5.8 What's the context?	15–20	20–25+	To help students to remember new structures and to raise their awareness of how the language was taught.	**80**

	Time (in minutes) in class	homework	Aims	Page
5.9 Things I need to remember	10+	30+	To make students aware of the vital areas of a new piece of target language	81
5.10 Which error do I make frequently?	15+	45+	To make students aware of errors they make repeatedly	83
5.11 A question I have	15–20+	30+	To allow the students to ask questions that they may feel hesitant about asking in class	83
5.12 What's the difference between …?	15–20	40–60+	To encourage students to think clearly about the differences between their own language and English	84
5.13 Quiz	10	15+	To review various tenses in a fun way and engage students in thinking about the language, as well as using it	85
5.14 Grammar jazz chant/rhymes	15–20	40+	To help students to memorize grammar structures as well as to help them to hear rhythm in English	86
6 Focus on communication				87
6.1 Structured conversation	15+	45+	To provide practice of language taught in class. To encourage the students to 'play' with the language and record the results of their efforts	88
6.2 Real life	10–15	40–60+	To encourage students to practise functional language outside class and to complete real-life tasks which will make homework meaningful	89
6.3 Beginner review	10	10–15	To help beginner students to develop their confidence, especially in their ability to remember words and use them correctly	90
6.4 Using cue cards	10–15	20–45	To encourage new learners to practise class-taught language orally in a way which will help them to memorize target language as well as develop accurate use of the language	91
6.5 Telephone calls	10–15	2–3	To help students gain confidence speaking on the telephone	93
6.6 Telephone whispers	10–15	1–2	To encourage students to speak in English on the telephone, and to improve their listening skills along with their speaking skills	94
6.7 Night-time questions	15–20	30–45	To encourage students to review language at any time of the day and to help them to memorize language, developing both fluency and accuracy	94

	Time (in minutes) in class	homework	Aims	Page
6.8 Taped journal	10–20	5–15	To encourage students to practise talking about a variety of subjects which are relevant to them. Also to encourage them to listen to themselves while speaking, so they can focus on their own accuracy along with fluency	**96**
6.9 Tape as a monitor	15–20	20–30	To encourage students to listen to themselves speaking English. This will not only develop their listening skills, but will also develop accuracy	**97**
6.10 Describe the picture	20–30	45+	To encourage students to prepare for oral presentations in class	**99**
6.11 The art gallery	10–15	60–80	To exploit an interest students may have in art and to use visual stimuli from outside class	**101**
6.12 A museum visit	60 minutes	60+	To encourage students to use the resources around them, e.g. museums and art galleries. Also to encourage the students to activate their English outside class as much as possible	**103**
6.13 Being a guide	10–15	60–80	To provide students with realistic applications of functional English	**104**
6.14 We're going to the zoo	10–15	60–80	To encourage the students to match an outside interest with the use of English	**106**
6.15 Create a role	40–50	20–30	To give students the opportunity to create roles for themselves and their classmates	**107**
6.16 Cultural differences	20+	60+	To expose the students to other cultures and to increase their understanding of how far-reaching English is	**109**
7 Focus on pronunciation				**111**
7.1 Collect a *schwa*	10–20	30+	To raise students' awareness of the frequency of the *schwa* sound	**112**
7.2 What is different?	10–15	30+	To make students aware of differences between English sounds and the sounds of their first language. This will help students to recognize areas which may potentially be difficult	**112**
7.3 Writing tongue twisters	15–20	40–45	To encourage students to practise problematical English sounds in a fun way	**113**
7.4 Phonemes	10	30+	To introduce the phonemic alphabet to students over a period of time	**114**
7.5 Transcribing sentences into phonemic script	10–15	45	To highlight connected speech	**115**

	Time (in minutes) in class	homework	Aims	Page
7.6 Find words with the same sound	10–15	40–50	To make students aware of the difference between spelling and the way words are pronounced	**116**
7.7 Write your own minimal pair list	10–15	40–50	To encourage students to concentrate on sounds they find particularly difficult	**116**
7.8 Marking stress in individual words	10–20	30–40	To make students aware of varying word stress	**117**
7.9 Collect patterns	10–15	30–40	To heighten students' awareness of varying word stress and to emphasize the value of dictionaries for learning outside class	**118**
7.10 Direct a partner	10–15	45+	To practise varying intonation patterns and heighten students' awareness of the need to use intonation to express emotions	**118**
7.11 Picture sounds	15	25–45	To focus on particularly problematical sounds. The pictures will also help more visual learners to remember the sounds	**119**
8 Focus on receptive skills				**121**
8.1 Let's go to the movies	10–15	10–15	To use students' enjoyment of the cinema to promote language learning	**122**
8.2 Notes from the news	5–10	20–30	To encourage students to listen for both general and detailed information using an authentic listening source	**123**
8.3 Listening to advertisements	10	20	To practise listening for detailed information using an authentic source	**124**
8.4 A scene from your favourite programme	30	40	To encourage students to listen for both detail and general information. Also to consider pronunciation, especially intonation, and how it is modified for the feelings in a scene	**124**
8.5 Transcribe a song	20	60+	To exploit material which students already listen to; to practise the ability to listen for detail	**125**
8.6 Song lyrics	15–20	30–50	To encourage students to listen to songs in English; they will also practise their writing skills as they will answer in complete sentences	**126**
8.7 Famous person	20	50–80	To encourage reading for detailed information about an interesting theme. To provide students with exposure to authentic materials	**127**
8.8 Dictate a puzzle	20–30	60+	To provide a clear reason for reading and listening—to work out the solution. The aim in class is listening for detailed information. The aim at home is reading	**128**

	Time (in minutes) in class	homework	Aims	Page
8.9 Jigsaw	10	45	To encourage students to read for general and detailed information, and to read authentic materials as much as possible	**129**
8.10 Find authentic material	15–30	40–50	To encourage students to find out about each other and to find a text they would like to read	**131**
8.11 Find the site	10–15	45	To surf the Internet in English rather than their first language	**133**
8.12 English in my town	10–15	45–60	To heighten the students' awareness of English in their own area	**134**
8.13 Vocabulary to teach my class	20–25	40+	To encourage students to be independent learners and to find out what is useful for them	**134**
8.14 Write your own comprehension questions	20	45–55	To provide practice in writing questions in English as well as reading for detailed information	**136**
8.15 Read the article!	30–40	30–40	To encourage students to read for a specific purpose, e.g. to develop an argument for a debate in class	**136**
8.16 Give out the headlines	10–15	30–45	To encourage students to read the news in English	**137**
8.17 Cultural awareness	20	30–40	To encourage students to find out about other cultures whilst practising their ability to read in detail	**138**
8.18 Gossip	20	45–50	To motivate students to read fun things in English	**139**
8.19 Baking	10–15	45–60	To provide students with a reason for reading. This activity is especially useful for students who enjoy doing, rather than simply sitting down and studying	**140**

Appendix: Useful websites for English learners 143

Bibliography 145

The author and series editor

Lesley Painter has been teaching English as a foreign language for over 12 years. She has taught younger learners, business students, general English courses and ESP courses in South Korea, Poland, Hong Kong, Portugal and the USA. She has given teacher training workshops in Europe and the USA to teachers of English as a foreign language. She is currently based in New York, doing teacher training and teaching. She has published various articles about teaching English as a foreign language and has also published a book of role plays.

Alan Maley worked for the British Council from 1962 to 1988, serving as English Language Officer in Yugoslavia, Ghana, Italy, France, and China, and as Regional Representative in South India (Madras). From 1988 to 1993 he was Director-General of the Bell Educational Trust, Cambridge. From 1993 to 1998 he was Senior Fellow in the Department of English Language and Literature of the National University of Singapore. He is currently a freelance consultant and Director of the graduate programme at Assumption University, Bangkok. Among his publications are *Literature*, in this series, *Beyond Words*, *Sounds Interesting*, *Sounds Intriguing*, *Words*, *Variations on a Theme*, and *Drama Techniques in Language Learning* (all with Alan Duff), *The Mind's Eye* (with Françoise Grellet and Alan Duff), *Learning to Listen* and *Poem into Poem* (with Sandra Moulding), *Short and Sweet*, and *The English Teacher's Voice*.

Foreword

*'Homework, groanwork,
Put it down and moanwork.'*

So goes a popular children's poem. Such unpleasant connotations of homework are indeed widely shared. Most of us can recall the acres of dreary exercises we were subjected to under the label of homework—and the desperate, and sometimes creative, excuses we found for not doing it.

Yet homework makes good practical sense, particularly in language learning. It is rare for students to have more than a few classroom hours per week. This is certainly not enough exposure to achieve proficiency in the language, even over the span of several years. If learning is to be effective, a good proportion of it must take place outside these few classroom hours. Setting homework is one of the best ways to achieve this.

Homework has the further advantage of being a different mode of learning from the classroom lessons. In the classroom, students are taught in a group, and are often required to learn in ways which may not suit their individual learning styles. They are also unlikely to get much individual attention, and may additionally come under peer pressure to under-perform. Work done alone, or occasionally in pairs or small groups, outside the classroom, is a different form of learning, where the learners can decide for themselves how to tackle the tasks, in ways which suit their own preferred modes of learning.

It is therefore refreshing to find a book on homework which departs radically from the dreary 'do the exercises on page 15 of your workbook' style. The activities in this book are based largely on finding out what learners like to do outside the classroom, and what they are capable of doing. In many of these activities, the students themselves are involved in the setting of their own homework tasks. This often involves them in choosing texts, and even in writing exercises for each other. The activities are usually quite short, and do-able. And the results often feed back directly into further activities in the classroom. So the homework is personalized, relevant, and even enjoyable!

The book offers a wide variety of sources for homework activities—film, radio, newspapers, songs, websites—rather than the tedium of trivial writing exercises. It also covers all major skill areas, including pronunciation.

This is the best available compendium of ideas for bringing homework in from the cold, and making it an integral part of the learning process, rather than a disagreeable appendage.

Alan Maley

Introduction

'Nothing great was ever achieved without enthusiasm.'
Ralph Waldo Emerson, American writer and public speaker (1803–82)

What is homework?

Homework is a vital part of learning, and it is expected by students, parents, school directors, and teachers. The benefits of homework are obvious: students retain class-taught language, they reinforce what they have learnt, they develop study habits which ultimately allow them to develop as independent learners, and their cognitive understanding of language increases.

Homework is an extension of the classroom which allows students to internalize information that has been presented in class. It bridges the gap between lessons, so that students can continue to work on English throughout the week even if they have only two classes a week. Homework is, therefore, a cornerstone of students' learning process. Most educators understand this and set homework conscientiously.

Both students and teachers can use homework to monitor progress. Parents can also do this. In their book *Seven Steps to Homework Success* (see Bibliography), Sydney S. Zentall and S. Goldstein explain the value of homework to parents: 'Homework is important because it is at the intersection between home and school. It serves as a window through which you can observe your children's education.'

The role of homework

Students themselves often fail to appreciate the fundamental role that homework can play in their education. Sarah North and Hannah Pillay, in their *ELT Journal* article 'Homework: re-examining the routine', report findings from a homework survey of Malaysian English teachers. They asked the teachers about the efficacy of homework, both in terms of how they as teachers dealt with homework and about the performance of their students. 'The results showed an interesting discrepancy, with many teachers reporting satisfaction with their own performance, but not with their students' performance. The overall impression was that a significant number of teachers feel they are doing the right things, but are not achieving the results that they would like.' North and Pillay quote the following comments from teachers: 'Students don't want to do their homework. They would rather copy, or get scolded by me.' 'At least half of them try to complete the work started in class, while the rest copy each other's work. Most of the students have the tendency to copy answers since they have too many other subjects.'

Many teachers can identify with these comments. I have always tried to set useful homework, and spend time designing valuable activities for the students. However, the results have often been that few students do the homework, many copy from the diligent students, and others make a joke of not handing in any work. We have all heard the age-old excuses for not giving in homework, such as 'the dog ate it', or 'I left it on the bus'. If this is a common experience in classrooms, homework needs to be re-evaluated as a classroom protocol.

Re-evaluating homework

A few years ago, at the end of a lesson, I opened my coursebook in order to set some homework exercises for the students. They looked at me dolefully, almost as though they were surrendering in a battle, and resignedly wrote down what I asked them to do. As I looked at my students I knew what the results would be. I wasn't wrong. When I collected the work from them in the following lesson, only half of the class had done it. Of the work handed in, every single answer was identical (probably originating from the strongest student in class). I knew that it would be difficult to motivate myself to correct their work.

I continued to set homework tasks, but I began to wonder why the students weren't more motivated. I decided to work on the issue by first identifying my own aims. I decided that I wanted to achieve the following:

1. Students should feel homework tasks are useful.
2. Tasks should be interesting and varied.
3. Work should include not only written tasks, but tasks focusing on all skills.
4. Individual students' needs should be met, which means varying homework tasks for different students.
5. Students' attitude to homework should be improved, for example, by allowing them to contribute ideas by designing their own tasks.
6. Language should be liberated from the classroom.

Before you continue reading this book, please take a few minutes to answer the following questions. You may like to consider them as part of a group activity with your colleagues.

1 Why do you, as a teacher, set homework?
2 How do you feel when marking homework?
3 Is the homework always in written form, such as gap-fills, compositions, etc.?
4 How much importance do you place on homework?
5 Have you ever asked your students what importance they place on homework?
6 Can you remember specific tasks that you have set for homework?

Now think about one class that you teach at the moment.

1 Do the students do their homework?
2 If they don't, why is that?
3 How motivated are they?
4 How long does it take to do the homework you set?

While answering these questions, I began to think about how I would approach homework as a learner and what I would like to do while learning. Doing things we enjoy is a vital part of homework. I was learning French and decided to set myself homework. I started by listing my own leisure activities:

- going to the movies
- watching television
- reading (usually fiction)
- talking on the phone.

I now had a set of activities that I could adapt as homework tasks. Next, I considered which topics interested me:

- famous people
- current events
- different cultures
- food
- health.

I designed this activity for myself based on the above findings:

1 Watch the French movie *Amélie* on video.
2 Pick out words that you know in French; pause the tape, repeat the language, and try to improve your pronunciation.
3 Write the story of *Amélie* in French.

The task was motivating because it was based on an activity that I wanted to do, i.e. watch the film.

In the next lesson with my students, I told them to go to the movies, watch a film, and write a summary of it for me. They also had to give the film a star rating (five stars being a must-see, no stars being a must-not-see). Of my 15 students, 12 did the homework—not bad. Students will do things which they enjoy. I also enjoyed reading their summaries.

Now think of a group of students you teach and answer these questions:

1 What interests do they have?
2 What would be the most interesting homework task that you could set them?

Set this task at the end of the next lesson, and see what the results are. Now reflect on how you can continue to motivate students outside class.

A new approach

In an interview with Glori Chaika for the *Education World* website (see Bibliography), Howard Gardner, the creator of the theory of multiple intelligences, said that: 'Teachers should devote energy to creating homework that is stimulating and provocative rather than banal. And parents or mentors should go shoulder-to-shoulder with youngsters, helping to motivate them, thinking of ways in which to help them without giving the answer, and being aware of the child's special gifts and weaknesses.'

In the booklet *Helping Your Students with Homework*, Sharon Bobbitt wrote: 'Homework is meant to be a positive experience which encourages children to learn. Assignments should not be used as a punishment.'

Both are talking mainly about children, but the same is true of adult students. If homework is seen as a punishment or as banal, it will not be effective. I experimented with homework tasks and found that they needed to meet the criteria below in order for students to do and benefit from the work.

1 Make it fun

Think about what your students are interested in—what do they do outside class? Do they read, watch movies, go out with friends? Then think about how these activities can be turned into homework tasks.

2 Make it relevant

For students to commit their time to homework they need to see its value. In class, we as teachers often signpost our work: *Now we are going to look at these words, because they will help you when you need to write a letter.* Students are aware of why we are asking them to do certain things. The same should be true of homework—we need to communicate the aims behind it. Consider asking students to watch a movie: *I'd like you to do this because it's fun, and because the lexis is up-to-date and useful.* It's simple, but it may mean that your students will understand the progression they will make in their studies by doing the work.

If we can convince students to do the work we set, all of the benefits that were mentioned at the beginning of this introduction will occur. Students will increase the pace of their learning and when their progress becomes obvious, they will be more motivated in class. In my experience, when this happens setting homework becomes increasingly easy because students are always more likely to do the work when they know they are benefiting from it.

3 Match students' learning preferences

Ultimately, homework creates an autonomous learner: someone who takes an active role in the learning process, generating ideas and taking advantage of learning opportunities. For learners to become autonomous they must recognize their own preferred ways of learning. As teachers we make available options for learning, and students have to make conscious decisions about what works for them.

Some learners are very self-aware and confident enough to follow their own path. Other students may need more guidance and support as they may hold onto previous learning experiences or misunderstand their own ways of learning. As teachers we can encourage students to continue to do activities which are successful for them, as well as to try new ways.

The following questionnaire will help to establish learner styles. Its aim is not necessarily to label the students (*you are a visual/kinaesthetic learner*) but to make students aware which types of activities they prefer, and encourage them to do what works for them—when and where it works best. If students can find out their preferences, they should be better able to facilitate their own learning outside class.

Ask the students to consider tips for themselves. You can then go over their answers in class and add more ideas and advice. Consider suggesting some of these points.

1. If students like to work with partners, encourage them to meet outside class. Recommend a place and time that they can meet. There may be people in class who already enjoy working together—exploit this by asking them to do certain tasks together and to write homework as a joint effort. This may not be as arduous as doing tasks alone.
2. If students enjoy music, ask them to decide on music which best fits with English studies. Students can come up with a list which they can display in class. You may want to recommend music too.
3. When students say they enjoy reading, find out what it is specifically that they enjoy. It may be science fiction, for example, or romance novels. Ask the students to bring in books they have read in their own language and ask them to describe the plots to you in English. They can prepare projects on their favourite authors and present information in class.
4. If students like to read aloud, ask them to record themselves. They can try reading a variety of different text types. Listen to the tapes and give them feedback on their speaking skills. Students could

also work on speaking activities from this book, which will capitalize on their enjoyment of speaking in English.

5 When students draw or doodle, it may mean that they like learning in a visual way. Involve these students in activities which use pictures or other visual tools.

Encourage students to make their own homework plan, giving the times and days when they will work. This is especially useful for exam students, and for business students who may be on a tight schedule.

Questionnaire

Where and when:

1 Do you learn better in the evening, morning, afternoon, or at night? (If you don't know, experiment.)

2 When do you have time for yourself so that you can study without distraction?

3 Where do you prefer to study: at home, at work, in the school library, over a coffee, outside?

4 Do you like to be in complete silence or with background noise, such as music?

How:

5 Do you like to complete exercises from a workbook or coursebook?

6 Do you like to create your own sentences and ideas?

7 Do you like to listen to English more than you like to read it?

8 Do you like to work with a friend?

9 Do you like to speak rather than listen?

10 Do you like to read aloud?

Give yourself a tip, perhaps by completing one of the following, if it applies to you:

I like to work with someone, therefore I should ______________________

____

I like to listen to music, so maybe I should ______________________

____

I like to read aloud, so I should ______________________

____

I like to be alone, therefore I should ______________________

____

Time

Students have to make a time commitment if they are to do homework. Of course, they have many external distractions: television, the movies, going out with friends, reading in their first language, and so on. Students who are also working or in school have many other time-consuming tasks. Therefore the activities we set need to be not only motivating, worthwhile, and enjoyable, but also manageable in terms of time. All too often, too much homework is set after a class, which can mean that even a motivating task becomes a lengthy chore.

In conclusion

This book addresses some of the problems that we, as teachers, face with homework and aims to provide useful, fun activities that can make homework tasks motivating. Experiment with what works for your students, rather than relying on more traditional ideas. If homework is to fulfil its place in the learning cycle, we first and foremost have to make sure our students do it, by making it reflect their interests and preferences, and fit with their time constraints.

How each activity is organized

This book is divided into skills areas and input areas, such as grammar and lexis. The format of each activity follows a similar pattern: it provides information on level, time, aims, preparation, procedure, and variations.

Level

This may vary according to the adaptations you can make. Generally the level given is the minimum for the activity. You know your own students best, however, and may feel that you can adapt the material for your group even if the activity is recommended for a higher or lower level. Look at the suggested Variations and Comments, where there may be additional material for a lower or higher level.

Time

The time heading indicates class time and homework time. This allows you to plan lessons around the activities. All the homework activities in this book include class time, as it is my aim to make homework a true extension of class work. Please note that the time needed may vary for different groups.

Preparation

This includes anything you may need to do before the class.

Procedure

This shows, in numbered steps, how to set up the activity.

Variations

These could be ideas on how to change the activity for different levels, or alternative ways of delivering the activities.

1 Getting started

You can begin the task of improving your use of homework by introducing the topic to the students and holding an open class discussion. Find out what the students think about homework, and make sure they are aware how much it can accelerate their learning. Then, using the questionnaires on pages 23–4, collect the students' considered opinions. These questionnaires will act as the foundation of your homework policy; the students should be aware of this and of the aims of the questionnaires. Make sure that, through discussion and the questionnaires, you collect enough information to enable you to make clear decisions as to the type of work you should set.

A group of business people I taught took a full week to collate the data they wanted to present to me. I then had sufficient information to make decisions about the work they could do outside class. I knew how much time they had available, and what sort of tasks they enjoyed and found relevant to their interests.

Armed with the completed questionnaires, you can look at the activities in this book which are relevant to your students' interests and needs. For example, for students who enjoy reading, look through Chapter 8 and set them varying tasks. If students say they enjoy speaking as opposed to writing and need to practise as much as possible, look at Chapters 6 and 7 and consider where and how the students can practise speaking English in your particular location.

Because you have spent class time and homework time negotiating a course of learning, students will begin to see homework is a valuable part of the lesson.

Working homework into your curriculum

Students should not feel that homework is haphazard or unfocused. They need to see it as a routine part of learning and understand its overall aim. They must also see its relevance to what they are doing in class. If they think it represents a last-minute decision by the teacher, students will be demotivated and therefore unlikely to do it.

Begin by looking through the questionnaires and the coursebook you have to cover. Match the students' requests to activities from the book and work them into the course of lessons.

Memory work

One of the most difficult things about English is the amount that students have to memorize. Some students may indicate this in class—I have frequently been told by adult learners that they are too old to remember a lot of new things. Encourage students to help themselves by using mnemonic aids. Ask them to do their own research into memory techniques. There are many websites that students could look at—see the Appendix to this book for examples.

Encourage students to make contact with English in their home towns. Place a local map in the classroom and mark places where they can hear or read English, such as: the library, a cyber café, the tourist information centre, shops selling English newspapers, and so on. Keep adding to it and encourage the students to try out the new places. This should continually motivate students to remain active when studying.

Dictionary skills

Encourage students to use learning tools and develop the skills necessary for homework, such as using a dictionary. A dictionary quiz like the one opposite will show them how much information they can glean from dictionaries.

Hand out copies of this quiz and ask the students to use it as homework with their English dictionaries.

For lower-level students, do the quiz in class and discuss abbreviations for parts of speech.

In class, discuss the value of dictionaries and how students can use them for a variety of purposes: to look up a pronunciation, a part of speech, a variety of English, etc.

You may want to expand pronunciation work by asking students to look up other words in dictionaries. You can begin to incorporate these into lessons. As much as possible, focus students on the relevance of knowing the sounds system. Providing the students with phonemic charts will help.

See *Dictionaries* by Jon Wright, in this Resource Books for Teachers series, for a wealth of ideas on making more effective use of dictionaries.

Quiz

1 Look up the word 'picture'. Which part of speech is it?
2 Can 'picture' be a verb?
3 Look up 'information'. Is it a countable or uncountable noun?
4 How do you know whether a word is countable or uncountable?
5 What is the abbreviation for 'adjective'?
6 What abbreviation is used for 'idiom'?
7 Find one idiom and write it down, with its meaning.
8 How can you write 'picture' phonemically?
9 On which page are all of the phonemic symbols in your dictionary?
10 Write the word 'information' and note how it is stressed, using your dictionary.
11 Look up 'labour'. What is the American spelling?
12 How do you know which words are American or UK English?

Monitoring homework and providing feedback

Feedback is one of the main motivating forces for students that keeps them doing their homework. Spend time considering the ways you give correction and feedback. In particular, make grading clear so that students can identify their progress and areas of weakness. Also, consider the type of dialogue that you can create with your students through their homework, i.e. via the comments you make on their work. Once you have begun a dialogue with students, ask them questions and make sure that they respond.

Look at the ideas below to help structure your thinking. Begin by encouraging students to keep their own records, in an exercise book entitled *My Homework Book*.

1.1 My homework book

Level All

Aims To make homework exercises as important as class tasks and for students to identify the aims behind homework tasks.

Materials An exercise book for each student.

Procedure

1 Ask the students to keep an exercise book only for homework. Tell them to leave the first two or three pages blank.

2 In class, ask the students to write *Contents Page* on the first page. Explain that every time they do homework they are going to note down on the contents page the task and the aim of the task, like this:

Contents page

Activity	Aim
1 Gap-fill	To practise the simple past tense

3 Students should keep their book up to date and review their work as often as possible.

Comments

You may want to keep your own log of what the students are doing in class, and your own homework log.

Follow-up

Set the students goals, for example, to complete a certain number of tasks or to work on specific areas where they are having difficulty. At the end of the course, award class prizes, including one for 'best homeworker'!

1.2 Correcting homework

Level All

Aims To encourage students to correct their own errors and to identify their own areas of weakness.

Procedure

Give students a piece of text which contains errors of spelling, tense, word order, etc. Ask them to work in pairs to correct it. Then ask the students to think of a code that the teacher can use to show the learners the correction that needs to be made. Ideas are:

Sp	Spelling
WO	Word order
T	Tense
Gr	Grammar

Pl Plural
Art Article

Use these symbols whenever you are correcting work. Put a poster displaying them on the wall of the classroom so that students can keep checking what the symbols mean. This is based on John and Liz Soars' homework code in the *Headway* series.

1.3 Comments to add to homework

Level All

Aims To add fun to the comments you write on homework, and to create a fun dialogue with your students.

Procedure

After you have finished marking a student's work, add a suitable comment to encourage and motivate, or to make him or her smile.

Examples
That didn't hurt, did it?
Awesome.
You did that surprisingly well.
It's good to see that you are listening in class.
This was well done. Your last homework was medium to over done.
A lot of work went into this—well done.
Congratulations on your first piece of homework.
As always, great.
A rare masterpiece.

To help students organize their own learning time at home, you may want to encourage them to set a certain amount of time aside for a particular amount of work to be done. Some students may do their work at the same time every day, or do 30 minutes a day at different times. It may be easier for students with busy schedules to do a little and often. Some students may work better if they work with others; it might help to pair people up in class, i.e. to recommend who works with whom. Some students may need to experiment with locations where they work best, for example, at the office, at home in their bedrooms, in a certain chair. Comfort is vital. Students should also remain goal-orientated and reflect on work they have done and their own achievements. This can be promoted in the ongoing dialogue you begin with them in your comments on their homework. For example: *I noticed in the first week you had trouble with the simple past tense, but now you're using it easily.*

Add variety to the ways you set homework, to make it more motivating for students. Consider trying the next two activities.

1.4 Sending homework home in an envelope

Level Elementary and above

Time IN CLASS 15 minutes

Aims To set homework in a different way, which will motivate students to do the work.

Preparation

Write out homework tasks on slips of paper and place them in envelopes, one for each student. Put the names of the students on the envelopes.

Procedure

1. Deliver the envelopes containing the homework instructions to students in class.
2. Tell them to open the envelopes at home.

Comments

If the group is particularly disinclined to do homework, different delivery tactics may help to motivate them. It's novel at least!

Variation

Send the homework tasks via email or snail mail.

1.5 Mission impossible

Level Beginner and above

Time IN CLASS 15 minutes

Aims To add variety to the way that homework is set.

Preparation

Write down sections of the rubrics for homework on pieces of card, and display them around the classroom.

Procedure

Ask students to collect the information to find out their homework task.

Variation 1

A twist to this activity is to tell the students that the first student to find out what the task is can be excused from homework for one lesson!

Variation 2

1. Write down the parts of a homework task on slips of paper. For example:

Review

Page 27 of the

coursebook

2 Hide the slips around the classroom and tell the students that they have to find each slip as quickly as possible. In order to find out exactly what the homework is, the students will need to gather all of the slips.

Comments

The last two activities make receiving the homework task more fun. They are especially useful with younger learners. Students can also set homework for their friends in the class. Consider the activity below.

1.6 Send a word via email

Level **Beginner and above**

Aims **To deliver homework via email.**

Procedure

1 If the students have email, get them to exchange email addresses, and give them the task of choosing a word in English for which they would like their friends to find out the meaning. Ask them to email a friend with a word they have found in the dictionary, heard in class, or read in a magazine.

2 Once the students have received words from their friends, they must find out the meanings of those words and reply giving the definition.

3 The students can take it in turns to continue this activity. If you have all of the students' email addresses, send words to each of them. Ask them to give the definition of these words in the next lesson.

Variation

If students do not have access to email they could exchange written or verbal messages.

Comments

1 This activity should also help to foster a community learning experience, where the students focus on their own improvement but also on that of their friends in class. This may help younger learners who need to have a group understanding of homework; more mature learners may also feel the benefit of support from their colleagues.

2 Keep asking the students how they study at home; they may have ideas which can help the group. This type of work will help to focus the students and to increase their efficiency of learning.

2
Focus on homework

The way a course begins forms a first impression; first impressions are usually lasting. The first impression you give to the students of the work that is to follow is likely to be remembered, so it's a good idea to make homework a part of the very first lesson. Show the students how you mean to go on, i.e. with regular work outside class. Sarah North and Hannah Pillay (see Bibliography 5) suggest that homework needs to be re-evaluated, and call for a change in the relationship between work at home and work in class. The first chapter of this book deals with bringing about such changes.

The first change is to place the focus on the students taking a greater role in deciding what work they will do outside class. Provide opportunities for them to contribute to the activities they will be asked to do. Use the questionnaires at the beginning of this chapter and then activities which the students themselves design and choose (Activities 2.2, 'My favourite task', 2.3, 'Design a homework task for your group', 2.4, 'Skills work', and 2.5, Letter to the new learners'). The questionnaires should reveal students' feelings and preferences about homework tasks, and once you have the results you can plan your course of homework tasks to take these into account. The first set of activities allows students to adapt tasks or recycle ones they have enjoyed doing in class. This should motivate them to be more productive concerning homework tasks and more aware of what works for them in terms of studying. The responsibility for setting work is thus shared a little more equally between teacher and student, and a more mature relationship is developed between learner and teacher—the learner is not only a receiver but also a giver. The classroom community becomes open to suggestions and the students, as a group, learn to help each other along with themselves.

The range of tasks can easily be matched to your curriculum as many can be related to whatever topic is being studied at the time. For example, Activity 2.2, 'My favourite task', includes deciding which tasks best help to learn language. Simply change the language skill that is being taught, and keep asking the students to think of tasks for themselves. Ultimately the students need to understand what you as a teacher expect from homework, but also (and more importantly) what they can expect to gain from it. Homework should be seen not only as something required by a teacher, but as work that is beneficial for students themselves.

In *How to be a More Successful Language Learner*, J. Rubin and I. Thompson say: 'unless you [learner] can take charge of your own language learning, you will probably not succeed in mastering the new language. You know yourself best, so you should use your self-knowledge to guide your studies.' This is a very useful starting point for a class discussion about being a learner. Homework is intended to help students to learn, but this is achieved only if the activity motivates them and suits their learning preferences. If students help you to help them, the learning cycle will be much more productive. All too often homework consists simply of activities and exercises that focus on restricted, repetitive practices which may not be memorable or meaningful. Make sure that your students see the importance of their input and encourage them to take responsibility.

2.1 Setting up homework

Level Pre-intermediate and above

Time IN CLASS 20–30 minutes per session (two sessions)
HOMEWORK 30–40 minutes

Aims To allow students to provide feedback on homework tasks, and say what they found useful and effective.

Preparation

Photocopy a questionnaire (see pages 23–4) for each student in class. Two questionnaires are provided. Your choice of which to do will depend on the amount of information you want from your students. All the questions are related to homework and homework tasks.

Procedure

1. In class, put the students in pairs and give each pair two photocopies of your chosen questionnaire. They should ask each other the questions on the sheet, and note down their partner's answers.
2. Ask the students as homework to read the notes their partner made of their answers, and to summarize their findings.
3. In the following lesson, ask students to discuss their feelings about homework based on their summaries.
4. At the end of the discussion, students should list activities they find useful and enjoyable. Prompt the students by suggesting activities, such as watching a movie in English, reading a magazine or surfing the Internet. By the end of the activity you should have a list of homework activities that you can set when teaching these students.

Comments

1. Feedback is to be used when setting tasks for the students, i.e. designing tasks that they like and will do. Students should feel they are taking an active role in contributing to their learning processes.

2 At this point in the students' learning, it would also be useful to ask the question: *What do you find difficult when studying English?*, as lower-level students may be able to indicate where they need help most. For example, I had a group of beginners who told me, in their first language, that they found the amount of vocabulary in class difficult to cope with. I therefore decided to spend time working on word cards (see Chapter 3).

Variation 1

Lower-level students could complete the questionnaires in their first language, and if necessary you could have the findings translated. (In my experience the administrative staff of schools have always been willing to help with translating.)

Variation 2

You can do the above entirely as a homework activity. Give each student a copy of the questionnaire and ask them to complete it for homework.

Follow-up

Collect the questionnaires and keep them so that you can set homework activities which the students have said they enjoy.
As you are setting tasks for homework, remind students what they wrote and what they said they enjoyed: *I'm setting the journal-writing task because you said that you did this in your own language—why not try in English?*

Questionnaires

Questionnaire 2 is concerned with what works for students, i.e. directing them to think about what best helps them to learn. By collecting this information you will be able to set the students tasks which will be effective for them as individuals. As Nunan wrote in *Language Teaching Methodology* (page 98), it's important to establish a link for the students between the task and its rationale, otherwise the 'learning how' dimension will be lost. Look carefully at the questionnaires and try to match activities to students' preferences. Continually ask for feedback about how useful or motivating the tasks were. Repeat activities that the students like, and avoid ones they don't enjoy.

Homework questionnaire 1

1 What types of homework does your teacher normally ask you to do?

2 Do you usually do your homework? If not, why not?

3 What do you do outside the classroom to help you learn English, for example, keep a vocabulary book, read magazines?

4 List tasks that you would really enjoy doing for homework, for example, watching MTV or watching the news in English.

2.1

Homework questionnaire 2

How I learn

1 How do you learn new vocabulary words in English?

2 How do you remember new grammar structures?

3 How do you learn the correct way to say a word?

4 What do you find really helps you to learn English?

5 If you had to take an English test tomorrow, how would you study?

What I want to do

6 What do you like to do in your free time?

7 What do you like to do in English, for example, speak to people, watch movies, or listen to songs in English?

8 Do you like surfing the Internet?

9 Do you like listening to the news in English?

10 Do you enjoy reading? If so, what?

11 Do you enjoy writing in your free time?
Do you write a lot of emails or keep a diary?

Finish this sentence:

If I were a teacher, I would ask the students to …

What's the most boring thing for you about studying?
What do you hate about being a student?

A completed questionnaire

Homework questionnaire 2

How I learn

1 How do you learn new vocabulary words in English?
Try to use new words with friends. Need to write them. Like someone to explain them. Don't like to use dictionary.

2 How do you remember new grammar structures?
When writing, review notes in notebook

3 How do you learn the correct way to say a word?
Ask a native speaker correct pronunciation and repeat

4 What do you find really helps you to learn English?
Read books about technology, watch TV in English

5 If you had to take an English test tomorrow, how would you study?
Review notebooks, course book, vocabulary

What I want to do

6 What do you like to do in your free time?
Watch movies, read, go to beach, go shopping

7 What do you like to do in English, for example, speak to people, watch movies or listen to songs in English?
Listen to songs

8 Do you like surfing the Internet?
Yes

9 Do you like listening to the news in English?
Yes—CNN

10 Do you enjoy reading? If so, what?
Poems, newspapers

11 Do you enjoy writing in your free time?
Do you write a lot of emails or keep a diary?
Trying to write poems in English. Some emails.

Finish this sentence:

If I were a teacher, I would ask the students to …
Say how to cook a special dish for parents' anniversary

What's the most boring thing for you about studying?
What do you hate about being a student?
No feedback. No interaction. Hate to memorize idiomatic expressions.

2.1

Decisions based on this questionnaire

1. I would suggest that this student works with a friend, as she said she likes to speak to a friend. Activity choices: 3.1, 'Use it!' She likes surfing the Internet, so also 3.2, 'Find examples of ...', using the Internet. 3.3, 'Words from the news' is also a good choice because she likes reading the news and watches CNN.
2. The student reviews her notes a lot so I would suggest that she makes sure she creates a contents page for her work. She likes being with a friend, so I would ask her to do 5.6, 'Let's experiment' with a friend, i.e. to use the language and record the response.
3. The student would probably benefit from listening to English more; I would suggest any of the listening activities in this book.
4. The student likes to read poetry, so I would suggest that she reads certain poets in English, such as Emily Dickinson. I would also suggest that she complete 8.7, 'Famous person', about this poet. Her research can be done on the Internet.
5. The student likes to go shopping so I would suggest 6.13, 'Being a guide'. She can visit stores and find out information for the class.
6. The student likes to listen to songs. I would suggest she complete 8.6, 'Song lyrics'.
7. The student does use the Internet so I would recommend websites she may be interested in, such as the CNN news site; 8.11, 'Find the site', would be an appropriate activity.
8. The student likes to listen to the news so I would suggest 8.2, 'Notes from the news'.
9. I would suggest any of the reading activities, because she enjoys reading.
10. The student likes to write, therefore I would encourage her to write poetry and also suggest 4.1, 'Diary'.
11. At the bottom of the questionnaire the student has noted that she doesn't get feedback. She means sufficient correction, so I would recommend 5.10, 'Which error do I make frequently?', to help guide her studies and to focus on correction.

2.2 My favourite task

Level Pre-intermediate and above

Time IN CLASS 10–15 minutes
HOMEWORK 30–40 minutes

Aims To motivate the students by doing activities they enjoy and to give them the fun of doing it all themselves.

Preparation

Choose the resources you would like students to use, for example, a text from the coursebook, an article from a newspaper or an activity from a workbook.

Procedure

1. Group the students into threes and ask the groups to think of one task an English language teacher has asked them to do which they really enjoyed, and felt was very effective for their learning. Brainstorm reading exercises, language activities, etc. Note the results, as you can use this for future reference when planning lessons.
2. Distribute the materials you would like the students to use.
3. Tell the students that they are going to have the opportunity to repeat their favourite activities in class, using the material you have given them. Their homework task is to prepare the activity themselves, and write down the procedure.
4. In the next lesson, collect their work; you may need to correct the work and you will also need to photocopy any materials the students will need.
5. Set aside time in lessons so that the students can do the activities they have designed.

Comments

1. I make this a 'last thing on Friday' activity. Every Friday I ask a student to present their activity and explain why he or she has chosen it. Then we do the activity as a group. The students find this highly motivating, and as we repeat the procedure over the months we are together, they become increasingly skilled at choosing useful class activities.
2. The activity especially helps to motivate high-level learners who would like to take control of their own learning. It is also especially suitable for English for specific purposes groups, and business students who may know exactly what type of activity they need to do in order to practise the skills they need. Students will begin to feel confident making their own decisions about how to learn, rather than relying on the teacher for constant guidance.

Variation 1

You may want to limit this to simple activities such as games or warm-ups and avoid the use of materials—simply ask the students to write down a procedure as homework. Allow them to direct the activity in class. A group of Brazilian students chose to do the following:

1. A warm-up using metaphors—the student asked us to stand up and say what colour we felt like at that moment.
2. A Beatles song—the student wrote out the lyrics, having obtained them from a website, and cut them up. He put the jumbled pieces on the floor and as we listened to the song we had to put the lyrics into the correct order.
3. A phonemic bingo game—using a dictionary, a student drew bingo cards with phonemes in the squares. I read out words that contained the sounds, and the students all crossed off phonemes as they heard them. The first student to complete a line correctly was the winner.
4. A vocabulary matching activity using cards—a word on one card and a definition on the other.
5. A vocabulary game, 'Backs to the board'—one student had his or her back to the board, I wrote a word on the board, and the other students had to guide the students to say the word, without actually saying it themselves.

Variation 2

Set specific aims for the students' activities. For example, if the class has just learnt adjectives to describe character, say to the students: *At home, think of a way to memorize these words*. If they have just studied the past simple, ask them to think of an activity which practises this. This is challenging, but remember that learners may have had many English lessons and therefore can think back to lessons they have had and activities that worked for them.

2.3 Design a homework task for your group

Level Pre-intermediate and above

Time IN CLASS 10–15 minutes
HOMEWORK 30–60 minutes

Aims To give the students the responsibility of creating a homework task for their class.

Preparation

Photocopy the worksheet below for each student in the class.

Procedure

1. During the last 10–15 minutes of a lesson, ask the students to think of homework tasks they have done which were beneficial. Note these on the board.

2 Give out the worksheet below and explain to the students that for homework they are going to design a 'super' homework task. Allow the students time to read the 'mission'.

3 Tell them to write down the procedure for the activity at home, and also to write down the reason for their choice of task.

4 In the next lesson, collect the tasks. Correct them and ensure that they are suitable tasks for the group.

5 Set the tasks for homework over the course of your lessons. Every time you do so, explain which student wrote the task.

6 Monitor the students' reactions to each task—did they like doing the task, was it motivating, useful, etc?

Comments

This helps students to take control of their own learning. It is also extremely helpful if, as was the case for me when I was working in Poland, you see the students only once or twice a week for a few hours. Helping them to bridge the gap between lessons by thinking of useful ideas will promote effective study skills and prevent the memory drain.

Variation

Group the students into threes and ask them to brainstorm homework activities they have done which they disliked. Then ask them to share their ideas with the whole class. For fun, tell them that if they can come up with a good reason why you shouldn't set that type of homework, you won't in the next few weeks. This is an activity that younger learners enjoy.

Mission: design a task

Your mission is to design a homework activity which you think will really improve your English. It should be something that you WANT to do and CAN do.

For example: watching a video in English and writing down new phrasal verbs that you hear; looking for information on the Internet; or listening to songs in English and transcribing the lyrics.

The activity must be fun, something that everyone will have time to do, and it should be creative! Then we'll set your classmates the homework!

Here are some activities that students in New York created:

Cartoons

Students brought into class some English cartoons regularly featured in a newspaper and asked other students to read them. They then asked the other students to think where they could see these cartoons, for example, in newspapers, magazines, etc. They set the other students the task of trying to find where the cartoons were featured. Over a period of one month the students kept looking for them. Whenever they found them, they brought them to class to read. They completed different homework tasks with the cartoons; for example, they decided which were the funniest and which were the cleverest, they wrote new captions for the cartoons, etc. A montage of the cartoons was put on the classroom wall for students to discuss and read. At the end of the one-month period, the students completed a homework assignment in which they gave their impressions of the cartoons, said who they appealed to, the type of humour they contained, etc. A competition was then set in class: to see who could write the best caption for one of the cartoons. The aim was to create a common interest in the group.

Movie

A class was divided into groups of four. Each group decided on a movie that they wanted to go to see. The only criterion given was that the movie had to be in English. The groups had to go and watch their chosen movie and take notes as they watched. Once back in class, the groups worked together to clarify the movie's plot and to compare their notes. After they had compared notes, they had to add false elements, for example, saying that the movie was set in America in the 1950s when in fact it was set in Japan in the 1940s. They then had to retell the plot of the movie to a different group; when they retold the story, they had to include the false elements.

The second group then had to go to see the movie they had heard described. As the students were watching, they had to check for the true and false parts of the report. This activity was based on a spot-the-difference activity students had done in class. It could also be done in class, using videos. See Activity 8.1, 'Let's go to the movies', for a variation on this task.

Dictionary work

A class was divided into groups of four. Each group wrote a list of five lexical items that they had previously been taught. They then designed vocabulary exercises that reviewed these words. Once the students had designed the exercises, they swapped their papers with other groups. Students had to complete the tasks—for example, gap-fill activities, matching activities, etc., for homework.

$2,000 for a day

One group of students gave other students in their class an imaginary $2,000 to spend on an evening out in New York. At home, the students had to decide what they would do with the money. When the groups were together in class, they described their ideal evenings to each other. As an extension to this, the whole class had to decide which was the best evening out from all of the suggestions, i.e. the ultimate night out in New York.

2.4 Skills work

Level Intermediate and above

Time IN CLASS 10–15 minutes
HOMEWORK 40 minutes +

Aims To allow students to bring activities to class that they find motivating and useful.

Preparation

Find a suitable reading text to use, either from the coursebook or an authentic piece of material.

Procedure

1. At the end of a reading lesson (receptive skills lesson), brainstorm different reading activities that have been done in class with the students. For example, a jigsaw reading task in which each student had a different section of the same text and had to explain his or her section to the rest of the group. Ask them which activities they enjoyed.
2. Tell them that for homework they have to design a reading activity. Give the students a copy of the reading text that you want them to use. They could replicate a type of activity they have already done, or invent something new, for example, something with a competitive aspect.
3. Ask them to write out the procedure for their tasks and to add reasons why they want their classmates to do them.
4. During the next lesson, collect the tasks. Correct the work and allow the students to present their activities and their aims in class. Set the new student-created tasks for homework, or do them in class.

Comments

This is useful for groups who are beginning to feel that the coursebook and class material are becoming predictable.

Variation

If students feel comfortable organizing their own activities, you could give them the option of creating a speaking or vocabulary review activity.

Follow-up

During this activity, the students' preferred learning styles will become apparent, as they will design tasks that reflect their own styles. After you have completed one of the students' activities, lead a discussion about how students feel they learn best, and what preferences they have when they learn.

2.5 Letter to the new learners

Level Pre-intermediate and above

Time IN CLASS 15–20 minutes
HOMEWORK 30–40 minutes

Aims To encourage students to analyse their success as language learners and to consider what helps them best when studying.

Procedure

1 In class, preferably in the middle of a course or of a school term/year, ask the students to evaluate their English language learning so far. Ask them what needs to be done in order to learn English, what is difficult about it, etc. This could be done as a whole-class activity in the last 15–20 minutes of class, or as pair work which you can monitor.

2 Put on the board two headings, 'Positive' and 'Negative', and brainstorm study tasks that were enjoyable/not enjoyable, effective/ineffective.

3 At the end of the discussion, ask the students for their homework to write a letter to an imaginary new student who is going to join the school or start learning English. Explain that the letter should contain practical help on how to learn English, along with tips and inspirational notes.

Ask the students to be specific about essential study skills that have helped them, and to focus on what to do outside class rather than inside class.

4 During the next lesson, collect the letters, correct them and photocopy them. Keep the copies for new students and display the originals around the classroom.

Comments

The students may find the inspirational notes useful. A class I had collected them in English and also translated them from their own language.

Variation

Deliver the letters to another class within the school, post them on a notice board in the school, or post some letters on to an English language learning website.

Follow-up

During the next lesson allow the students time to read each other's letters. If there is time, have a discussion about the contents of the letters and about effective learning. If the students have added inspirational notes, write them on a separate poster or make a collage and pin it up in class. Ensure students have an opportunity to explain what their phrases mean. This display should help students to feel motivated to learn.

When new students start learning English, give them copies of the letters and ask them to reflect on the advice that has been sent to them.

Examples **Letter**

Dear New Student

For me reading newspapers and books is very helpful to learn English. I think this is a very good way to get to know a lot of new vocabulary and learn how to use and write it.

I also like to watch TV, listen to music and English tapes.

When I study new things I always write them down and put them on my wall.

Good luck,

From,

Alicja.

Inspirational notes

If you think you can, you can.
Life is a lesson.
Don't give up, there is an end!
If you worry about what others think of you, you won't do anything.
To have a rainbow you have to have rain.

2.6 Teach someone

Level **All**

Time IN CLASS **15–20 minutes**
HOMEWORK **60–90 minutes**

Aims **To help students to learn through teaching others.**

Preparation

1 Choose some language items that you would like students to teach each other:
- with low-level students it could be food items, or things around the house
- with higher levels it could be a language structure, or lexical items.

2 Photocopy the worksheet below for each student and then write on the photocopy what you would like the students to teach.

Procedure

1. Explain to the class that you would like them to teach a few English words to a friend, partner or family member. Tell them that they must be thorough when teaching—they must provide pronunciation work, give practice, check understanding, check spelling, etc.
2. Hand out the worksheet. Ask the students to do their teaching for homework and then to ask their learner to sign once they have completed the activity.

Items to teach ______________________________

____

How did you teach? ______________________________

____

____

Were you a successful teacher? ______________________________

____

____

____

Learner's signature ______________________________

3. When back in class, ask the students to describe how they taught the language and whether they were successful teachers.

Variation

Beginners should not be asked to complete the worksheet; you may also need to translate what you would like them to do.

Comments

It is well recognized that we all learn and retain information more efficiently when we teach what we have learnt to someone else.

Follow-up

Younger learners may teach their parents or friends. If they do so, you could arrange for the parents and friends to come into class to demonstrate what they were taught. This makes the task more meaningful because there is a result and an audience at the end. It is to be hoped that the parents and friends will enjoy participating in the class.

2.7 Homework excuses

Level Pre-intermediate and above

Time IN CLASS 45–50 minutes (optional)
HOMEWORK 30–40 minutes

Aims To show the students that the teacher knows all of the homework excuses already!

Procedure

1. Put the students into pairs and ask them to think of the worst excuse they have ever given to a teacher for not doing their homework. Remind them of the classics: 'My dog ate my homework!', 'The house was burgled and the robbers took it!'
2. Ask the students to recount these excuses to the whole class.
3. For homework, ask the students to think of the best excuse ever. They should write it down and bring it to the next class.
4. Collect and correct the work.
5. In the following lesson, hold the 'Best Excuse Oscar' award ceremony. Ask the students to say their best excuses in front of the whole class. If they are particularly brave, they can act out giving the excuse to a teacher, using their best dramatic skills. Decide on the best, and then give the student an 'Oscar'.

Comments

This activity is good fun. It also shows students that you understand that learning a language requires a great deal of commitment, which at times is hard to maintain.

3

Focus on lexis

Regular revision of vocabulary is important. As teachers we invest a great deal of time in lexical teaching and we need to spend an equal, if not longer, amount of time reviewing the students' lexicon in order for them to internalize the language. This involves experimentation, usage, analysis and ultimately adoption into the students' language. Possibly the students' own time (homework) is more fertile for vocabulary work, as it is free from the time constraints of lessons. Work done outside class on the task of knowing a word can be developed in many ways: through usage, analysis, experimentation, recognition in various contexts, to the end result of adoption.

Usage

After I had read H. G. Widdowson's book *Aspects of Language Teaching* for the first time, a poem by Emily Dickinson, which he had quoted in his book, remained with me as a reminder of a primary goal for language teaching—that students should put language to use. That poem inspired many of the 'Use it'-type activities in this book.

> A word is dead
> When it is said,
> Some say,
> I say it just
> begins to live,
> That day.

The first activity in this chapter is concerned with the most fundamental area of lexical work: encouraging students to use what they have learnt in class. This will help prevent 'avoidance', i.e. students not using the word because they rely on others that they already know. Students explore the uses and register of the language and experiment. When students work independently they will have to find out for themselves how successful their language use is, which means the process of using the language will be both memorable and valuable as a learning experience.

Finding examples

The second activity develops autonomous learning, as it requires the students to find examples of language on their own. This theme runs throughout the book, and throughout this chapter especially. To encourage students to work autonomously and gain varied exposure to language are the two primary goals of this chapter. The greater the exposure, the more likely students are to understand the language in use and to adopt it. Words do not exist in isolation. Setting tasks in which students look at words in context helps to provide them with clues as to meaning and function.

At the end of this chapter, various activities are included in which students identify a variety of forms of lexical items. I feel that this gives the English language a richness for students.

As always, keep an open dialogue with your students on the activities you do, as this will help you decide which activities to choose.

The news

When one of my students first began to listen to and watch the news in English, he said he felt that he was becoming part of the English-speaking community. Accessing the news is vital for students. News in itself is quite motivating for them; they probably already keep up with the news in their own language. Tapping into this interest, as the third activity in this chapter does, will act as a stimulus to developing up-to-date lexical items.

Memory

Consider work you can do to help students to remember lexical items. They often ask for ideas and suggestions—give some, and tell the students to be experimental. Here are some ideas that I have used.

1 Visual memorization: Ask the students to sit quietly and think over the words they have been taught. Ask them to repeat the words over and over to themselves, mantra-like, and to visualize their spelling. Ask them to do this repeatedly at home.
2 Word association. In *Inside Teaching*, Tim Bowen and Jonathan Marks list various association techniques, including the following:
   a Association with a mental image or picture. For example, mind maps or diagrams:

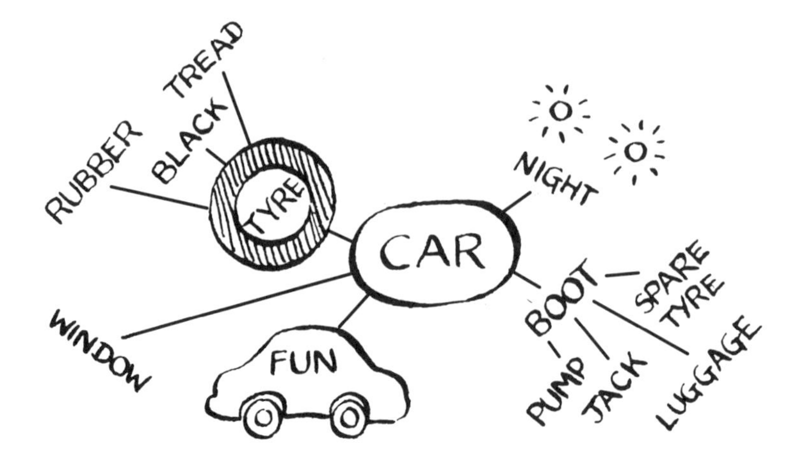

b Association with a situation, topic or story. Students try to remember the words in a particular context, for example:

BEACH: laughing — smiling — relaxing — playing — swimming

This could also be by association with another word, for example:

BLACK: midnight
BLUE: day

3 Think of something special about the word you want to remember. I learnt the difference between stalagmites and stalactites by remembering the following:

Stala**G**mite: *G* ***g****rows up from the* ***g****round.*
Stala**C**tite: *C* ***c****omes down from the* ***c****eiling.*

4 Learn the first letters of words in a lexical set and make them spell something. For example, I learnt the digestive system by memorizing a nonsense word made out of the initials taken in order:

MOSDICRA: Mouth, Oesophagus, Stomach, Duodenum, Ileum, Colon, Rectum, Anus

5 Visualize the words with a picture or diagram:

Bomb Terrorist Capture Terror

Suggest various ways to help your students, and keep asking them to experiment.

3.1 Use it!

Level Elementary and above (the level is determined by the lexical items you use for the activity)

Time IN CLASS 10–15 minutes
HOMEWORK 40 minutes +

Aims To ensure that students use language from the class and gain confidence in speaking English.

Preparation

Choose a list of idiomatic expressions for the students to focus on, and write these on slips of paper. There should be one for each student in class. See the examples below for lexical items that can be used.

Procedure

1 At the end of a lesson, give each student an idiomatic expression on a slip of paper. Ask them to find out the meaning of the expression for homework, and to use the idiom in a conversation either with another learner of English or a native English speaker. Remind them that they need to consider the formality or informality of the language and in which context it is used.

Examples
What's up?
How's it going?
Let's go and grab a bite.
I feel under the weather.
Let's stay in touch.
Could you lend me a hand?
I feel really down in the dumps.
I'm broke.
Will you drop me a line?
Can you figure out what the teacher wants us to do?
Could you put in a good word for me with the teacher?
Take the weight off your feet!

2 Ask students to note down the responses they receive when they use the expressions.

3 During the next lesson, the students should tell each other the responses they received. For example, for 'What's up?' the response may be: 'Nothing, just chillin'.'

Follow-up

Keep repeating this task; use lexical items that arise during lessons. Each time they do the activity make sure that the students keep a record of the responses received. By doing this you will know that they are using the language in a communicative way.

3.2 Find examples of ...

Level Pre-intermediate and above

Time IN CLASS 10–15 minutes
HOMEWORK 40 minutes +

Aims To expose students outside class to lexical items taught in class.

Preparation

Decide on specific lexical items that the students should try to find in use. This will be in line with what you have taught in class.

Procedure

1 Ask the students to look outside class for specific types of lexical items that have been taught. Students can look at the Internet, English newspapers, magazines or, if they are in an English-speaking country, at posters and billboard advertisements. (See the Internet resources listed in the Appendix.) Ask the students to find about three or four words/phrases. See the examples given below.

Lexical item types to look for

Euphemisms	*passed away, heavily built*
Multi-word verbs	*get into, get onto, get up to, get down to, get around to*
Compound nouns	*post box, bus stop*
Idiomatic expression	*take a break, that's that*
Slang	*no way!*

2 Once the students are back in class, ask them to show their examples, explain what the lexical items mean, and say where they found them.

Comments

Exposure to lexical items in authentic settings will not only be memorable but will also show students the relevance of what they are learning.

3.3 Words from the news

Level Intermediate and above

Time IN CLASS 20–30 minutes
HOMEWORK 30–40 minutes

Aims To expose students to lexical items which are currently in use in world English, while also making the language of the news more familiar to them.

Preparation

Watch the news so that the stories the students hear will be familiar to you.

Procedure

1 Ask the group to watch the CNN news or access any other English-speaking radio or television news, or real audio via the Internet. Ask them to listen closely to one story in particular, and to pick out one lexical item which may have been repeatedly used in the story, for example, *terrorism*, *cover-up*, *disaster*.

2 At the beginning of the next lesson, the students should tell each other the story they listened to and the word(s) they picked out.

Comments

If you do this activity repeatedly over a period of time, the students will practise their listening skills and gain confidence in listening to English. If the students find it difficult to begin with, reassure them that they need to pick out only one word in the story, and if necessary they can refer to the news story in their native language news programmes.

Variation

You can prepare your students for listening to the news at home by pre-teaching lexical items in class time.

1 Different methods can be used when pre-teaching the vocabulary. For example, give each student a card with a word associated with the news written on it, and ask them to provide the meaning of the word by looking it up in a dictionary. Go through the meanings together as a group.

2 Ask students to watch or listen to the news and to listen for those particular words.

3 In the following lesson, ask the students to go over what they heard when they watched the news.

Examples Words to pre-teach:

bomb	terrorist	crime
victim	peace talks	attack
thief	innocent	skirmish
natural disaster	hijacking	murder
kidnapping	turmoil	

3.4 English bag

Level Beginner and above

Time IN CLASS 15–20 minutes per session
HOMEWORK 15–20 minutes per session

Aims To create an effective way of storing new vocabulary items which is accessible, portable, and convenient for the students.

Materials

A bag or plastic wallet which can be hung in the classroom. Small pieces of card.

Procedure

1 At the end of a lesson, give each student a small piece of card and ask them to write one word or phrase from the lesson on the card.

2 For homework ask the students to write a sentence on the back of their card which contains that word.

3 Hang a bag on the wall in the classroom. In the next lesson, ask the students to mingle and show each other their cards. Collect the cards and check that the meanings and sentences are correct. Place these cards into the bag and show the bag to the students. Tell them that you will keep adding to the bag as the lessons continue.

Comments

This idea is helpful for students who feel overwhelmed by the amount of lexical items they need to learn.

Variation 1

If the students are familiar with the phonemic alphabet, you can ask them to add the phonemic spelling to the cards. They can obtain this from their dictionaries.

Variation 2

The students can keep their own bags of words. Younger learners enjoy this and can keep reviewing the cards with a friend or family member at home.

Variation 3

Beginning and lower-level students can be given cards with words already written on one side. Ask the students to write one antonym for the word on the back of the cards at home, showing them an example if necessary. In the following lesson, check the antonyms and then use these cards as prompts when drilling the students with different language structures, or use them in word card games—the students could be put into two teams, the word cards spread out in front of them, and each team should take it in turns to point to a card and call out the antonym for the word.

Follow-up

Keep doing the initial task over the course of your lessons, i.e. handing out cards and asking students to write down lexical items from the class on one side and sentences in which they are used correctly on the other side. The cards can be used in a variety of ways, for example:

1. At the beginning of a lesson, read out the lexical items from some of the cards. The students should call out definitions for the words as quickly as they can. You could make this a team game with the class in two teams. Read out a word from a card and then give one point to the team who can give the definition first.
2. Organize the class into two teams. Throw some of the words from the bag onto the floor. One member from each team runs and takes one of the words back to his or her team. The teams must try to put their word or words into another correct sentence (in addition to the one on the back of the card) as quickly as possible. As soon as they have a sentence, they should call it out. The first team to do so correctly scores a point. Then the next two students should run and take words. The team with the most correct sentences wins.
3. Take out a card and give a definition of the lexical item to the students. They should then call out the word or words as quickly as possible.

3.5 Word review

Level Beginner and above

Time Homework 50 minutes +

Aims To have fun reviewing lexical items while also concentrating on how the words are spelt.

Preparation

Photocopy a word square for each student in class (see below) or get the students to draw it.

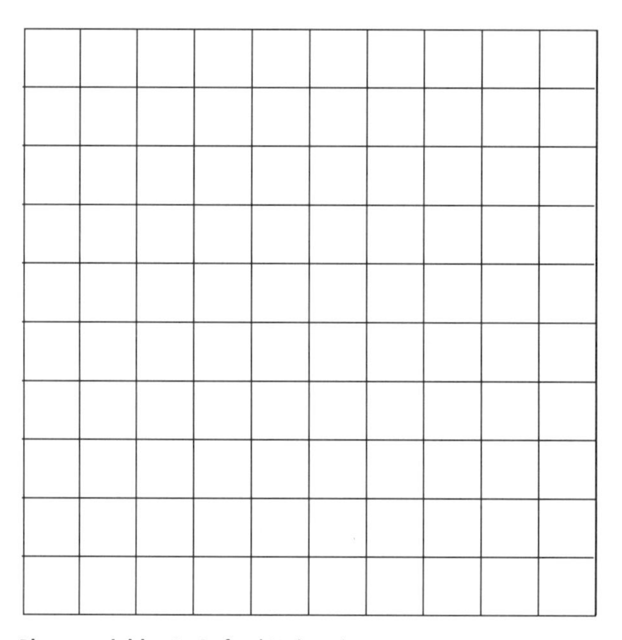

Photocopiable © Oxford University Press

Procedure

1 At the end of a lesson, preferably at the end of a week, give the students copies of the blank word square or ask them to draw one, For homework, ask them to try to fit as many words as possible that they have been taught in class onto the grid. They should write one letter per box. The letters must go from left to right in the first line and then from right to left in the second, and the last letter of each word must be the first letter of the following word. All the words must be complete, and students should try to use all of the boxes.

Example the words HELP PLAY YESTERDAY YET TALK would be entered as:

H	E	L	P	L	A	Y	E	S	T

The grid should be made smaller for lower-level learners, so that there are fewer boxes to fill.

2 In the following lesson, collect the grids and check them.

Follow-up

For a warm-up at the beginning of a lesson, give the students their grids back and ask them to read their words out as quickly as they can—it's not easy! Time the students with a stopwatch for fun.

3.6 Word box

Level Elementary and above

Time IN CLASS 10 minutes
HOMEWORK 40 minutes +

Aims To heighten students' awareness of spelling and to allow them to have fun with words.

Procedure

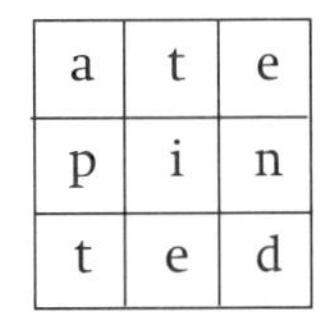

a	t	e
p	i	n
t	e	d

1 Draw the word box on the right on the board, and show the students how words can be read diagonally, horizontally and vertically.

2 Set the task of fitting different words into the box for homework. Explain that the students needs to decide on their own three-lettered words.

3 In the next lesson, collect the students' word boxes to check and draw a blank grid on the board. Organize the students into pairs and ask each pair to draw their own blank grid in their exercise books. Read out the words from one or two of the grids and ask students to decide how to fit them in the grid. The first ones to fit them successfully should call out.

Comments

Students who are particularly analytical may enjoy this challenge.

Variation

Make the box bigger by adding more squares, so that students must find four-lettered words.

3.7 Finding examples of collocations

Level Intermediate and above

Time IN CLASS 10–15 minutes
HOMEWORK 60 minutes +

Aims To increase students' exposure to collocations and to make them consider collocations in context.

Preparation

Decide on the types of collocations you would like the students to look for. If using visuals, photocopy enough for the class.

Procedure

1 To introduce this activity, ask the students to match verbs and nouns that collocate, and ensure that they are familiar with collocations.

Examples

Take	a photograph, medicine
Have	a cup of tea, a cold, lunch

Alternatively, write some nouns on the board and ask the students to work in pairs to think of a verb which precedes them all.

Examples

[Make]	[Set]
a date	the table
a bed	the date
a stand	the clock
a fool of himself/herself	

2 Ask the students to find two or three other examples of collocations outside class. Tell the students to look in various authentic resources, for example, on the Internet, in magazines, on television, etc. You may want to restrict the types of collocations that the students look for by genre or by construction, i.e. verb + noun, noun + noun, adjective + verb, adverb + verb.

3 During the next lesson, the students should share their examples and the meanings of their collocations.

Variation

Ask the students to find collocations in news items.

Follow-up

Give the students a picture of a situation and ask them, as homework, to find collocations associated with this situation.

Example

Collocations for a courtroom scene

to plead guilty, to be found innocent, to press charges

3.8 Looking at advertisements

Level Intermediate and above

Time IN CLASS 30 minutes +
HOMEWORK 30–40 minutes

Aims To expose the students to language used in advertisements, and to help students feel confident when faced with authentic materials.

Preparation

Find an advertisement from the television, a billboard, magazine, or newspaper, which contains interesting language such as a pun, phrasal verb, an idiom, or slang.

Procedure

1 At the end of a lesson, show the students your example of an advertisement that uses interesting language. Tell them how useful advertisements are for providing examples of a variety of lexical items.

2 Ask the students in pairs to decide the following about your example:
- What is being advertised?
- What does the language in the advertisement mean?
- What is the target group for the advertisement?

3 For homework, ask the students to look at advertisements in English, and specifically at the language. Ask them to find three advertisements which have the type of lexical item you want them to focus on (for example, a phrasal verb or an idiom). The students should either bring the advertisements into class or write down the advertisement's language. Advise the students where to look.

4 At the beginning of the next lesson, give the students large pieces of paper and ask them to write down the language they found.

5 Display the papers around the class and ask the students to walk around the room and to try to work out the meanings of the new language, and what is being advertised.

Follow-up

At the end of the activity, students could vote on the most effective advertisement. Ask the students to look at advertisements regularly, and occasionally to bring them into class in order to show other students.

3.9 Collect false friends

Level **Intermediate and above**

Time **IN CLASS** **15 minutes**
HOMEWORK **60 minutes +**

Aims **To make students aware of false friends and to help them to avoid the pitfalls they pose.**

Preparation

Find examples of false friends in the first language(s) of the students you have in class (if necessary, colleagues will help you to find a useful list).

Procedure

1 At the end of a lesson, write a few examples of false friends onto the board, for example, *sympathetic* (French), *nervous* (Polish), *confident* (French), *actual* (German).

2 Ask the students to think of the meanings of these words in their own language and in English. Ask the students why they are called false friends. Then instruct the students to look for one or two examples of false friends as homework.

3 In the next lesson, ask the students to present their examples. They should explain the meanings and you can help them model the pronunciation. Write the examples on posters and display them in the classroom. The posters will then act as a constant reminder for students to avoid using these words incorrectly.

Variation

Ask the students to find one English idiom which translates into the same or almost the same terms in their own language. For example, 'to be pulled onto the carpet', meaning to get in trouble with your boss, is almost the same as a Russian expression. Ask them to research the etymology of the idiom. They can do this by using the Internet or library resources. They could do the research in their own language, and then translate it for class.

Follow-up

Make this homework an ongoing task and add to the poster whenever the students find more examples.

3.10 Match the expression with the day

Level Pre-intermediate and above

Time IN CLASS 15–20 minutes
HOMEWORK 50 minutes +

Aims To review set expressions that are used on certain occasions in various cultures; to provide an opportunity for students to find out about other cultures and to express information about their own.

Preparation

Find out the national holidays and special festivals that the students in your class celebrate. Copy a list of English expressions connected with festivals and holidays that you'd like the students to use in their homework activity. The example below shows common Western festivals, but the students may be asked to focus on US, Australian or British days as a way of learning about other cultures.

Examples
Happy Valentine's Day
Happy Mother's Day
Happy New Year
Merry Christmas
Many Happy Returns
Happy Birthday
April Fool!
Happy Halloween
Trick or treat?
A pinch and a punch for the first of the month
Happy Easter
Happy Father's Day

Procedure

1 List the months of the year on the board, asking the students to help you, and then ask them, in pairs, to think of special days in the year.

2 Listen to the students' feedback, and write down their suggestions under the correct month.

3 For homework, hand out your list of expressions and ask the students to find out when these phrases would be said.

4 In the next lesson, go over the students' answers at the beginning of the class.

Follow-up

Ask students to think of a special day in their own culture. Ask them to write about that special day and translate the expressions they might use on that day. Collect the work and display it on the classroom walls. Allow time during lessons for the students to read the work.

Variation

Give higher-level students this questionnaire on set expressions to complete at home. In the following lesson, go over the answers with the students and ask them to discuss the differences between what you say in English and what you say in their own languages.

1. What do you say on someone's birthday?
2. What do you say when someone has had a baby?
3. What do you say when someone is going to take a test?
4. What do you say before you drink alcohol with someone?
5. What do you say when someone sneezes?
6. What do you say when someone looks unhappy to make them feel better?
7. What do you say to someone who is unwell?
8. What do you say to someone when it is his or her wedding anniversary?

Answers

1. Happy Birthday/Many happy returns of the day
2. Congratulations
3. Good luck
4. Cheers
5. Bless you (although many English-speaking people prefer to say *Gesundheit*, which is German and non-religious)
6. Cheer up
7. Get well soon
8. Happy anniversary

3.11 Body language

Level Intermediate and above

Time IN CLASS 10–15 minutes
HOMEWORK 30–40 minutes

Aims To present students with thematically related idioms. To make these expressions memorable by using visual aids, and to encourage students to keep using visuals when reviewing vocabulary.

Preparation

Cut up slips of paper (one for each student in the group) and write down the name of a body part such as *leg* or *arm* on each one. Draw the outline of a human body on poster paper and pin it up in class.

Procedure

1. Give each student a slip of paper naming a body part. Ask the students to find idiomatic expressions for homework which name that body part, and to write these on their slips. Advise the students to look through their notebooks from class, use dictionaries, and search through magazines, newspapers, and the Internet.

Examples He's really getting under my skin.
She's all fingers and thumbs.
He's put his foot in it.
She's had her nose put out of joint.
He's all skin and bones.
He elbowed his way in.
She's always splitting hairs.
There were a lot of raised eyebrows over the decision.
She gave him the eye.
By the skin of your teeth.
He got his foot in the door.
He's got her under his thumb.
It was a hair-raising experience.
She can wrap him around her little finger.

2. Once back in class the students should present their lexical item to the class with the meaning, and then pin the slip of paper to the body poster on the wall. This should make the lexical items memorable, as the poster will be a constant reminder of the language.

Variation 1

This activity can be also done with idioms using the names of animals, or colours.

Variation 2

1. Give the students slips of paper with idioms naming body parts written on them. Ask the students to find out the meanings for homework, using the various resources already mentioned.
2. When the students come back to class, ask them to define the idioms and explain where they found them.

3.12 Doubles

Level Upper-intermediate and above

Time IN CLASS 10–15 minutes
HOMEWORK 40 minutes +

Aims To make students aware of this particular type of lexical item and to introduce them to an interesting aspect of English.

Procedure

1 At the end of a lesson, write a few examples of words used twice in an expression or idiom on the board. Explain the meaning of the expression and then ask the students to note the repetition of the language. Ask the students if this type of repetition happens in their own language.

Examples
Enough's enough
That's that
Time after time
A deal's a deal
A promise is a promise
What's done is done
When it's over, it's over
She goes on and on and on
He said it over and over again
He took it apart piece by piece
Day by day I felt better

2 For homework, ask the students to find two or three further examples of language with repetition in it, or give the students specific examples to define and to find in use.

3 In the next lesson, ask the students to discuss with their partners where they found the language and what the lexical items mean.

Comments

This is an especially good idea for students who have been learning for a long time and are feeling demotivated or bored.

3.13 Oxymorons

Level Upper-intermediate and above

Time IN CLASS 15 minutes +
HOMEWORK 60 minutes +

Aims To present oxymorons to students, to add interesting lexical items to the students' vocabulary and to motivate the students with interesting words and expressions.

Procedure

1 At the end of a lesson, ask the students whether they know what an oxymoron is. If they don't, put a few examples on the board (see the list below) and ask the students to try to work out what the definition of an oxymoron is. Ask the students for their answers, and then explain that it is a contradiction in terms.

Examples

Act naturally	Passive aggressive
A definite maybe	Friendly fire
Black gold	Almost exactly
Peace force	Deafening silence

2 For homework, ask the students to find more examples of oxymorons. There are several websites which list them—see the Appendix of this book for site addresses.

3 In the next lesson, ask the students to exchange their oxymorons (with meanings) with other students in the class as a warm-up.

Variation 1

1 Instead of asking the students to look for oxymorons, ask the students to look for idioms or expressions which contain a person's name (see examples below). Set the students the task of finding more examples and their meanings. Alternatively, dictate some expressions using names and ask students for homework to find out how and why they are used. Again, suggest websites and other research resources for the students.

Examples

Uncle Sam	Plain Jane
Joe Bloggs	Bob's your uncle
Even Stevens	I'm all right Jack

2 When back in class, collect the examples and display them. Allow time in class for the students to tell each other how the examples they found are used. Ask the students whether this happens in their own language, and if so to give examples.

Variation 2

Choose other types of language that the students could look for in English, for example, Shakespearean phrases or foreign words and phrases. The students could be asked to decide which they are interested in, and to find examples to report back to class, with meanings.

Follow-up

Ask the students to give examples of oxymorons in their own languages. Develop this into a discussion about oxymorons. For further homework, ask the students to create one oxymoron of their own in English. Discuss them in the next lesson.

3.14 Palindromes

Level Upper-intermediate and above

Time IN CLASS 10 minutes +
HOMEWORK 60 minutes +

Aims To have fun with lexical items, and also to focus on spelling.

Procedure

1 At the end of class write a list of palindromes on the board and ask the students whether they can see anything special in the list.

Examples

deed	madam	race car
level	pip	eye

A palindrome can also be a complete sentence, such as 'Madam I'm Adam.'

2 If the students cannot see the connection, either ask them to work on it for homework or write the word 'Palindrome' on the board and explain that this means a word spelt the same forwards and backwards. For homework, ask the students to find more examples.

3 During the following lesson, ask the students to discuss the words they have found.

Follow-up 1

Keep this activity ongoing, and at the end of the teaching term offer a prize to the person who has contributed the most palindromes to class.

Follow-up 2

Younger learners may want to make a collage of their words, or add them to an ongoing list displayed in class.

3.15 Crosswords

Level Pre-intermediate and above

Time IN CLASS 20 minutes
HOMEWORK 60 minutes +

Aims To ensure that the students go over lexical items at home in terms of spelling and meaning.

Preparation

Photocopy a crossword grid for each student and draw one on the board.

Procedure

1 At the end of a lesson, ask the students to tell you what a crossword is. Tell them that they are going to create a crossword at home with the lexical items that they have learnt in class.

2 Give each student a crossword grid and then demonstrate by writing a word on the grid on the board and brainstorming with the students a clue that could be written in order for someone to guess that word.

3 In the next lesson, collect the students' crosswords and check them. Make sure that the clues really show the meanings of the words. If not, correct or question them.

Across
1 2 letters
2 5 letters
7 4 letters
10 3 letters
11 4 letters
12 3 letters
14 6 letters
15 2 letters

Down
1 5 letters
3 3 letters
4 3 letters
5 6 letters
6 7 letters
8 6 letters
9 5 letters
13 3 letters

Comments

Crosswords are universal and many students enjoy them in their first language, so they will probably find this activity motivating.

Follow-up

In the following lesson, organize the students into pairs and give them clues that a classmate has written and a blank crossword. Ask them to try to complete it. This activity could also be done as homework.

Answers

4

Focus on writing

Writing is a difficult skill even for native speakers. Unlike spoken English, written English lasts—once it has been put on paper it is there to be read and re-read. This is one of the reasons why we like to get it right. It shouldn't be a hurried task; time is needed to process it, edit it and produce something that can be understood easily by another person. As Tricia Hedge put it in her book *Writing* in this series, good writing includes:

- getting the grammar right
- having a range of vocabulary
- punctuating meaningfully
- using the conventions of layout correctly, for example, in letters
- spelling accurately
- using a range of sentence structures
- linking ideas and information across sentences to develop a topic
- developing and organizing the content clearly and convincingly.

For language learners this can all be daunting; however, it is also rewarding and helps to improve students' English in a variety of ways. It helps them focus on correct sentence structures, on spelling and punctuation, and on the form of certain tenses. It is a creative outlet, and allows students to reflect, experiment, make mistakes, and find solutions to problems.

In this chapter I have tried to develop ideas which motivate students to write outside class. In the first activity students are encouraged to write journals, which I feel is a useful task with clear guidelines as to content. Students do not need to be creative, just realistic. The exercise of writing down thoughts about events experienced each day is an invaluable way to evaluate what happened and to reflect. When you begin this activity you may want to ask students to think about what diary writing entails and what its benefits are—linguistic and non-linguistic.

Other activities are focused on using motivating prompts, for example, activities 4.9, 'My photograph', 4.11, 'Creative questions', and 4.13, 'Pocket stories'. The overall aim is to persuade students to write more outside class, because I agree with Tim Bowen and Jonathan Marks when they say in their book *Inside Teaching* that it is a 'forgotten skill'. They go on to say: 'With limited classroom time and limited time for correction of written work, anything more than a piecemeal approach will … occupy time that could perhaps be spent on more immediate linguistic needs.' I know that from personal experience, as I have prioritized speaking activities in class. Therefore, spending homework time on writing addresses the imbalance of skills. Do you spend enough time on writing in class? Look over this chapter and experiment with these homework activities with your students.

4.1 Diary

Level Pre-intermediate and above

Time IN CLASS 15–20 minutes
HOMEWORK 60–90 minutes +

Aims To encourage students to write a diary in English in their free time.

Materials

Photocopied or cut-out pictures representing the professions listed below, or others of your choice.

Procedure

1 At the end of class, ask the students to imagine being a famous person, a successful scientist, etc. Write on the board:

The doorman at a 5-star hotel
A nurse
A teacher
A chef in a busy restaurant
A pop star
A driver for a famous person
A successful scientist

If images of these are available, display those also.

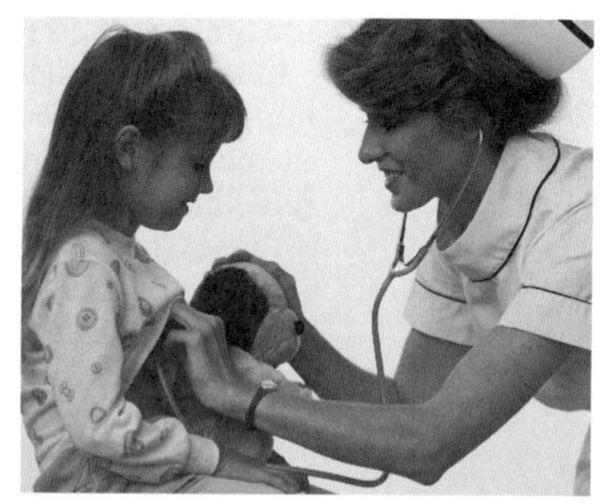

2 Organize the students into groups of three and ask them to discuss what it would be like to be one of the above people for a day. They should think about their daily routines and what kinds of things happen to these people. The students should end by telling the whole class about their group's discussion.

3 Ask the students to write a one-day diary entry for the person, based on their discussions, for homework. Prompt them to be creative and imaginative.

4 In the following lesson, collect the work, correct it and then display it in the classroom. In the next lesson, allow the students time to read each other's work.

Variation 1

If students are interested in history, ask them to write a diary entry as if they had been a witness to a historical event. To begin this activity, hand out copies of the diary entry (below) of a person who lived through the assassination of President Lincoln (US President, 1861–5). Don't tell the students what the person is describing; ask them to read the entry and decide what event it is talking about. Ask the students to imagine what it would have been like to be a witness to such an event. For homework, ask the students to choose one historical event, research it, and then write a diary entry.

April 15, 1865 Diaries of Rubens Peale (1784–1865)

... sad news of the murder of President Lincoln, he was shot while attending a performance at Ford's Theater last night in Washington. The assassin entered his private box and shot him in back of his head and then escaped, the assassin's name is —. The corpse arrived this afternoon from Harrisburg ... it was dark, even though the square was brilliantly illuminated with *greek lights* each side of the great walk ... It made a most brilliant appearance and lit up the whole square ....The crowd was so dense in Walnut Street that the police could scarcely keep the crowd back.

Source: *The Smithsonian Institution Archives of American Art*

Variation 2

Ask the students to write about the same event or time, collect all of their diary entries and make them into a newspaper. This activity could also be done using class time for the research. If you have the use of a computer lab with Internet access, you could take the students there to research a historical event. This research can then lead on to the writing activity above.

Follow-up

Encourage the students to begin writing a diary in English at home. Prompt them to write about current events along with their own personal notes. Tell them that they should show you the diary only if they want to.

4.2 Letter in a capsule

Level Pre-intermediate and above

Time IN CLASS 20–30 minutes
HOMEWORK 50 minutes +

Aims To encourage students to write letters in English, developing their letter-writing skills especially as to letter format.

Materials

A large glass jar or other container that can be buried as a 'time capsule'.

Preparation

Photocopy a letter like the one on the next page to use as an example.

Procedure

1 Start the activity by explaining to the students that they are going to write a letter that will possibly appear in history books years from now.

2 Give higher-level students copies of the letter as an example. Point out the date and explain that it is from the time of the US Civil war. Ask the students to read it and tell you some of the information that it gives us about that time and how the author felt.

3 Brainstorm ideas about who the students would like to write to. This could be a friend, a member of their family, the president of their country, etc. Remind them that this letter may be read in the future, so it needs to be clear and well written.

4 Also brainstorm the kinds of subjects that the students would like to write about, for example, their daily life, current events, etc.

5 Ask the students to write this letter for homework, thinking carefully about the structure of the letter and what type of language they will use—for example, set phrases, formal or informal language.

Aug. 17th 1862

Dear Wife,

Since I have left home, I have written two letters to you, but have not received one. I sent one by W. Hooper and one by Reuben Devereux. I looked for an answer last night, but was disappointed not to get one. I want to know how you are getting along. I was on guard last night for the first time since I have been here. George Devereux is very sick at the hospital. Mark Hatch and John Blodgett are there, but not very sick. The talk is now that the 16 regiment is going to leave here Tuesday morning for Washington. I don't know how true it is. I suppose that you have received that order for the town bounty. I sent it by J. Wilson. I have received all of my bounty, 85 dollars in all. I think I shall send it by express to you Monday. I shall send 80 dollars. I should have sent the whole, but I had to buy a pair of flannel shirts that cost me $3.50. The ones the government furnishes are nothing but white cotton. I went to the city to get my photograph taken, but they had so much to do I could not get a chance. I want you to get yours and Freddie's taken and send them to me. I will get mine taken the first chance and send it to you. Jack Jarvis expects Charles here tomorrow to carry home his things. I shall put my pants and shirt in the same box and direct them in care of Ithiel. Does little Freddie ask where I am? … Kiss him for me. I received a testament from Mason's wife. I sent the one you let me have home, because it was larger to carry. I have signed that allotment bill. I signed 10 dollars to be sent to you and the other 3 dollars will be paid to me. I shall try and get along with that much. The 10 dollars will be sent to the town treasurer and he will do it faithfully. You must write me all about the affairs at home and how you are getting along. I shall write every chance I have and you must do the same. You must not let anyone see this. It is written so poor. I don't have a very good chance to write. You must not worry about me. I shall try and take good care of myself as long as I am able. Give my love to all and receive a share yourself from your affectionate husband.

W. B. Butler

Source: www.resourcehelp.com/butler_1.htm

Follow-up

In the next lesson, collect in the letters and correct them. Then ask the students to place their letters into the capsule and, as a group, bury it in a suitable place. We hope that people in the future will find the letters and read them!

4.3 Exchanging letters

Level Elementary to intermediate

Time HOMEWORK 50 minutes +

Aims To encourage students to write letters in English, using a framework.

Preparation

Photocopy the gap-fill letter below for each student.

Procedure

1 Tell the students they are going to write a letter with a framework acting as a guide. Give the students this gap-fill letter to complete for homework.

2 In the following lesson, collect in the letters and correct them. Send them to students in the class, i.e. swap the letters between the students. Ask the students to write a reply, in English, to their classmate for homework.

[Address]

____

____

____

[Date] ________________

Dear fellow student,

How ________ you? I ________ fine. I am ________ a great time. Yesterday ____

____________. The weather is ________________. Today I ________________

____

Wish ____________ were here!

Lots of love, ________________

Follow-up

Suggest that the students continue to write letters or emails in English. They could send letters to other learners of English and start a pen pal/key pal relationship.

4.4 Most romantic love letter

Level Pre-intermediate and above

Time IN CLASS 15 minutes
HOMEWORK 40 minutes +

Aims To encourage students to write in a fun genre—i.e. romance, a genre that is very easy to identify with and effective for motivating students.

Preparation

Photocopy the love letter opposite for each student in the class.

Procedure

1 In class, ask the students to think of the most famous couples in history or literature, for example, Antony and Cleopatra, Romeo and Juliet. Ask them to imagine the kinds of love letters that these couples may have written to each other. The students could discuss this in pairs.

2 Give the students the example of the love letter opposite from Napoleon Bonaparte to Josephine. In pairs, the students could discuss the emotions expressed.

3 For homework, ask the students to write a love letter. Tell them it should be romantic and beautiful.

4 In the next lesson collect the letters in, correct them and display them in class—but remove the students' names in order to prevent them from being embarrassed.

Comments

There are plenty of websites with examples of famous love letters. If the students find this activity motivating, ask them to find other examples of love letters by famous people, which they can bring into class for the other students to read.

Variation

For lower-level students, hand out the photocopy of the love letter outline on the next page and ask the students to fill in the gaps.

Follow-up

Keep setting letter-writing tasks in class and keep varying the type of letter: for example, a thank-you letter; a 'Dear John' letter (to a boyfriend/girlfriend telling him or her that the relationship is over) a letter of complaint, etc.

4.4

Paris, December 1795

I wake filled with thoughts of you. Your portrait and the intoxicating evening which we spent yesterday have left my senses in turmoil. Sweet, incomparable Josephine, what a strange effect you have on my heart! Are you angry? Do I see you looking sad? Are you worried? ... My soul aches with sorrow, and there can be no rest for your lover; but is there still more in store for me when, yielding to the profound feelings which overwhelm me, I draw from your lips, from your heart a love which consumes me with fire? Ah! it was last night that I fully realized how false an image of you your portrait gives!

You are leaving at noon; I shall see you in three hours.
Napoleon

Source: www.theromantic.com/LoveLetters

To my ____________________,

I love you like the ____________________.

I love you more than ____________________.

I think about you ____________________.

You remind me of ____________________.

You smell of ____________________.

Your eyes are like ____________________.

When I am near you I feel ____________________.

When I am not near you I feel ____________________.

I ______________ wait until I ______________ you again!

Love,

____

4.5 Expand the story

Level Intermediate and above

Time IN CLASS 10 minutes
HOMEWORK 35 minutes +

Aims To help students to expand notes into prose; in turn, this should help students to take notes efficiently.

Preparation

Photocopy the notes below for each student in class.

Procedure

1 At the end of a lesson, ask the students what the aim of note taking is (to take down the most important information). Ask them when they need to do this. Explain that this activity will practise that skill.

2 Give the students copies of the notes from a news story. Ask them to expand the notes into a full story for homework. For example:

> Notes:
>
> Scientists found gene—gene defends against HIV infection. Hope: lead to better treatments. Current treatments becoming impotent. HIV affects gene CEM15 by producing protein. When protein removed, CEM15 OK—can fight HIV—stop HIV replicating. Study: Prof. M. Malim, King's College London + team from Univ. Pennsylvania. Malim said: 'Opens door for new treatments.'

3 In the following lesson, collect in the stories to correct.

Variation

For lower-level students, dictate or write on the board an outline of a short anecdote, such as in the notes below. Ask the students, for homework, to write about the events in continuous prose.

1 Restaurant—movies—my friend—last night. Movie terrible—ate Chinese food—lost keys—slept outside. Cold. Police woke me. Now feel tired.
2 Met friend last night—saw Tom Cruise. Tom Cruise very handsome —signed autographs—spoke to me!
3 Got up late—missed bus—felt poorly—boss angry—went home late—ordered pizza—asked my friend over.

4.6 Most unusual facts from the day

Level Intermediate and above

Time IN CLASS 15–20 minutes +
HOMEWORK 50–60 minutes +

Aims To encourage students to read outside class, and to practise note-taking skills.

Procedure

1. Give the students some newspapers, magazines, or downloaded pages of news from the Internet.
2. Ask the students to look as quickly as they can at the pages and find the *strangest* or *weirdest* story.
3. The students should retell the stories that they have found to other students in the group.
4. For homework, ask the students to find a *strange* or *weird* story in the news, take notes about it, and bring the information to the next lesson.
5. As a warm-up during the next lesson, ask the students to exchange their notes.

Variation

Give each student a different story type to look for—for example, the happiest story, the funniest story, a sports story, etc.

4.7 This was the day that …

Level Intermediate and above

Time IN CLASS 10–15 minutes
HOMEWORK 40–50 minutes per session

Aims To encourage students to research and present information.

Preparation

Photocopy an almanac entry for each student in class (see the example on the next page).

Procedure

1. Give the class the copies of the almanac and discuss with them the interest value of this material—for example, awareness of history, interesting facts, etc.
2. Tell the students that they are going to research a certain day in history for their homework, and create an almanac entry. This day could be, for example, the anniversary of Princess Diana's wedding, their own birthdays, or any other special occasion. The students can look at the Internet, visit the library, etc. Recommend suitable websites (see the Appendix) for examples. The students can use

resources in their own language also, but they must write the information for the class in English, possibly in the format of the original almanac that they were shown.

3 The students should exchange the information they have found at the beginning of the next lesson.

4 Correct the written work and display the articles in the classroom.

Example

ALMANAC March 28th

Famous birthdays:	Lucy Lawless (actor) Neil Kinnock (politician) Lesley Painter (teacher and writer)
Events:	Meltdown at Three Mile Island, 1979

Comments

Lower-level students could do all the research in their first language and translate the information into English.

4.8 Scrapbook

Level Pre-intermediate and above

Time IN CLASS 20–25 minutes
HOMEWORK 45–50 minutes

Aims To encourage students to write, read, speak, and listen to detailed information.

Materials

A few sentimental objects you would like to show the class, for example, a family photograph, a special piece of jewellery, a special souvenir, a letter, etc.

Procedure

1 Start this activity in class by showing the students a few items which are important to you and which represent special times in your life. Ask the students to look at the objects and try to guess why they are important to you. Once they have had time to discuss this, explain to them exactly what each object's sentimental value is.

2 Organize the students into pairs to discuss important items they have, to which they attach a sentimental value.

3 Tell the students that the whole class is going to make a scrapbook. Each student should bring an important object to class. Ask them to decide on objects they could bring, but advise them not to bring valuable items or documents that could get lost or broken—a picture of an object or photocopy of a document could be brought instead. For homework, students should each write a short paragraph about their item, explaining what it is and why it is important.

4 In class, ask the students to show their objects and explain them.

5 Assemble the objects in the class. If possible, photograph each object with the owner standing next to it or holding it. The pictures and descriptions can be collected in a scrapbook, or alternatively displayed on the wall.

4.9 My photograph

Level Elementary and above

Time IN CLASS 20 minutes
HOMEWORK 40–60 minutes

Aims To provide the students with a stimulating personal prompt.

Materials

A camera you can take into class, with enough film to take a picture of each student.

Procedure

1 In class, take a photograph of each student.

2 Develop the pictures and distribute a photo of a classmate to each student in class.

3 Ask the students to write about the person in the photograph for homework. The students can include appearance, personality, and interesting facts they know about the student.

4 In the following lesson collect in the photos and the descriptions. Correct the descriptions and then display them with the photos so that the students can read each other's work.

4.10 Pass the story

Level Intermediate and above

Time IN CLASS 20–25 minutes
HOMEWORK 20-minute sessions over three to four weeks

Aims To make story writing a collaborative experience; the result is a story created jointly, with plenty of anticipation and fun.

Procedure

1 Tell the students that the class is going to write a collection of stories, in parts and over a period of time. Start by brainstorming the information we need in order to write a story:

- type of story
- characters
- a time, for example, the future, medieval times, etc.
- a location.

Also discuss the fact that stories have

- a beginning
- a complication or problem in the middle
- an end or resolution
- a possible twist at the end.

2 Ask each student as homework to decide on a type of story, characters, a time, and a location. They should write a short paragraph about how the story begins.

Example A futuristic story taking place in 2050. It's set on Mars and has three characters: a robot, a monster, and the monster's pet. It's an escape story—they all want to escape from Mars.

3 In the next lesson, collect in the students' work and redistribute it so that each student receives someone else's work. Ask the students, for homework, to write the first half of the story they have been given.

4 In the next lesson, collect in the work and correct it. Redistribute the work to different students again and ask them as homework to write the conclusion of the story they are given.

5 If the students enjoyed this task, repeat the process and ask them to add a twist this time.

Comments

This activity can also be done in class instead of for homework. The students should work in pairs and after each stage the story should be passed around to different pairs. The advantage of this type of joint creative writing activity is that it doesn't put individual students under pressure to be creative. If they do the task at home, they have time to think and prepare, but when the activity is done in class students feel more relaxed, as they don't have to write large amounts of prose alone.

Follow-up

At the end of the activity, display the stories around the classroom so that the whole group can read them.

4.11 Creative questions

Level Pre-intermediate and above

Time IN CLASS 10 minutes
HOMEWORK 30 minutes +

Aims To focus students' writing and to personalize their work by using the students' names in the stories.

Preparation

Make photocopies of the questions below for each student and write your students' names in the gaps.

Procedure

1 Hand out a copy of the questions to each student. As homework, ask them to answer the questions.
2 Remind the students that that this is a creative writing activity, so they should be imaginative and have fun answering the questions in whatever way they want to.

Creative questions

Why was ______________ looking nervous in the last lesson?

Why did ______________ start laughing in the middle of the last lesson?

Why did ______________ smile at ______________ all lesson?

What did the teacher say to ______________ which was surprising?

What did ______________ say to ______________ at the break in the last lesson?

What did ______________ do to make ______________ laugh?

Why did ______________ and ______________ sit next to each other last lesson?

What did ______________ see out of the classroom window last lesson?

3 In the following lesson, ask the students to show each other their answers. Correct the work and then display it in class. Allow the students time in class to read each other's work.

Variation

Students can write their own questions, similar to the ones above, which you can use in subsequent lessons. Collect the questions, correct them and then set them either in class or for homework for students to answer.

4.12 Something you would write on a public wall

Level Intermediate and above

Time IN CLASS 10–15 minutes
HOMEWORK 40 minutes +

Aims To use a fun aspect of writing which is familiar in all cultures. It allows the students to be especially creative with the English language.

Preparation

Photocopy the list of graffiti below.

Procedure

1 Hand out copies of (or dictate) the examples of graffiti below. Organize the students into pairs and ask them to guess where this language could be found.

Examples
Give peace a chance
Make love not war
Billy was here
Free Ruritania

2 Ask the students to think of graffiti that they have seen. For homework ask each student to write a piece of graffiti in English.

3 Collect the examples and display them on the wall so that they can be read by all of the class.

4.13 Pocket stories

Level Pre-intermediate and above

Time IN CLASS 15–20 minutes
HOMEWORK 30–40 minutes

Aims To help students write a story using prompts.

Materials

Three ordinary objects (such as a diary, a bunch of keys, a pen) in your pocket or bag to show the students in class.

Procedure

1 At the end of a lesson, organize the students into pairs and ask the students to take out three things from their pockets or bags—encourage them by taking things from your own.

2 Ask the students to write a six-sentence story which includes the three items from their partner's pocket or bag.

3 In the next lesson, ask the students to read their stories to their partners.

5

Focus on language

One of the most fundamental expectations that students have of homework is that it will contain grammar exercises—and yes, it does. These exercises should reinforce structures that students have learnt in class and which are necessary to convey meaning.

How students learn grammar and begin to use it is a subject of great discussion among linguists and teachers of English as a foreign language. In *Language Teaching Methodology* David Nunan writes: 'The notion that learning is a linear, step-by-step process has largely been replaced by an organic, even metaphorical, view in which the development of grammatical competence is seen in terms of process as well as product.' H.G. Widdowson states that 'grammar is not just a collection of sentence patterns signifying nonsense, but something for the learner's brain to puzzle over' (*Aspects of Language Teaching*).

Homework and class activities need to allow for an organic process of language learning and allow students to 'puzzle over' language. The activities in this chapter try to reflect this process. It contains consciousness-raising activities and discovery activities. There are also activities which focus on form in order to reinforce structures. And in line with concepts mentioned before in this book, there are activities which encourage students to use the language outside class.

The most important thing to foster is an active enjoyment of the learning process. Gap-fill or information exercises may become monotonous, although they are useful. Vary activities and allow students actively to use language in context.

5.1 Find examples of ...

Level Intermediate and above

Time IN CLASS 10–15 minutes
HOMEWORK 40 minutes +

Aims To encourage students to search outside class for target language that has been taught. This activity should provide the students with realistic exposure to the language.

Preparation

Decide on a piece of target language that the students should look for and then prepare a worksheet using examples similar to the ones on the next page, containing examples of this language.

Procedure

1 At the end of class, ask the students to focus on a specific piece of target language which you have taught recently, such as the past simple or present continuous.

2 Ask the students to give you examples of the structure, and then hand out the worksheet.

Example
1 I've eaten sushi.
2 I've tried to learn to ski.
3 I've played tennis.
4 My friend's been to France.
5 I've just seen my friend outside.
6 We've studied English for two months.
7 I've already been for lunch.
8 I've lived here since 1997.

3 Set the students the task of finding examples of the target language on the handout. The examples must be the same as the ones on the worksheet in form, meaning, and use. The students can search the Internet, look in magazines or listen to radio or television programmes and then report back in class what they found and where they found it.

Variation 1

Provide students with a list of specific places that they should look for the language, for example, a news programme in English or MTV.

Variation 2

Younger learners could be asked to cut out the examples of the target language from their magazines or newspapers or download them from the Internet and bring them into class. A collage can then be put together showing the language they have found; this will make the task more memorable.

5.2 Make your own gap-fill

Level Elementary and above

Time IN CLASS 15–20 minutes
HOMEWORK 40 minutes +

Aims To vary the usual grammar book/workbook activities by giving students the responsibility of creating their own worksheets.

Preparation

Find a gap-fill exercise and photocopy it for each student or find one in the course book that you can show the students. This is only an example of what the students have to do.

Procedure

1 Give the students the photocopy of a gap-fill exercise or ask them to look at one in their course books. Ask them to tell you which grammar structure it is practising, and why these types of exercises are useful.

2 Tell the students that for homework they are going to write their own gap-fill exercise, using a target structure which you want them to practise.

3 Ask students to write out 10–12 sentences using the target structure, and then remove the target language. Remind the students to be creative when writing the sentences. They could use students' names from class, famous people's names, or write sentences about contemporary issues.

Example Complete using future forms:

A new president of the US ____________ elected.
Juan ____________ to university.
Carlos ____________ married next year.

4 During the next lesson, collect the gap-fills from the students and correct them. Then hand them out to different students and ask them to complete the gap-fill exercise at home.

Variation

1 The students can also make their own version of a 'find someone who' exercise. Ask the students to write ten sentences using the tenses specified by you.

2 Collect in and correct the exercises and redistribute them as homework for other students in the class.

Sentence 1: use the simple past
2: use the future simple
3: use the present simple
4: use the present continuous for the future
5: use the present perfect
6: use a comparative
7: use a superlative
8: use the second conditional
9: use the past continuous
10: use the simple past and the past continuous

Find someone who

1 went on holiday last year.
2 will go out tonight.
3 lives in an apartment.
4 is working on his/her homework tonight.
5 has been to Japan.
6 has longer hair than me.
7 is the tallest in the class.
8 if they had enough money, would travel around the world.
9 was watching the television until 10 p.m. last night.
10 was watching the television while he or she did homework.

5.3 Truths about my class

Level Pre-intermediate and above

Time IN CLASS 20 minutes +
HOMEWORK 40 minutes +

Aims To encourage the students to share information that they know about each other using class-taught language.

Preparation

Decide on the target structure that the students should use.

Procedure

1 At the end of a lesson, ask the students quickly to review the target language they have been learning.

2 For homework, ask the students to write true statements about each student in class using the target language. For example, if the future perfect had been covered in class, the students should think of statements about each student's future.

Example *By the end of this year:*
Ludmila will have finished building her house.
Mickey will have moved back to Korea.
Marcin will have got married.
Yumiko will have had her baby.

3 When the students come back into class, they can mingle and read out their sentences, checking their accuracy.

Comments

Keep repeating this exercise using the various language structures you are teaching. In my experience, students like to write about one another and ask to repeat this activity.

5.4 Rhyming simple past

Level Elementary to intermediate

Time IN CLASS 5–10 minutes
HOMEWORK 30 minutes +

Aims To revise simple past irregular verbs.

Preparation

Photocopy the list of simple past irregular verbs below.

Procedure

1 Give each student a copy of the simple past irregular verbs list and ask them to find other simple past irregular verbs that rhyme with each word.

Simple past irregular verbs
slept ______
met ______
did ______
lost ______
wore ______

Examples wept, crept, leapt
set, let
hid
cost
saw

2 Collect the work in the next lesson. Discuss the verbs and then, in following lessons, as a warm-up or at the end of class, call out irregular verbs and ask the students to call out others that rhyme with them.

Comments

The verbs can be varied according to the level of the students.

Variation

This activity can also be done using present participles and past participles.

Examples

leaving	weaving	spoken	woken
trying	dying	laid	paid
going	rowing	walked	talked
talking	stalking	fought	bought
playing	straying	moaned	loaned

5.5 Colour the text

Level **Elementary and above**

Time IN CLASS **15 minutes**
HOMEWORK **10–15 minutes**

Aims **To review various tenses in a memorable way. This may help students who find visual techniques effective when learning.**

Preparation Find a suitable text using various tenses (like the example on the next page).

Procedure

1 Give out the text at the end of the class. Tell the students that they are going to colour-code the text. For example, ask them to colour the present tenses in red, the past tenses in blue, and the future tenses in green. Work through an example in class.

2 In the following lesson, collect the texts and check whether the students have identified the structures correctly. This is especially useful if you want to check that students have understood what you have taught.

Vietnam's vanishing primates

I NEVER thought my wildlife tour of Northern Vietnam would begin in a zoo. But last November, when I visited the Cuc Phuong National Park, 75 miles south of Hanoi, I discovered that most of the animals I'd come to see—Vietnam's unique gibbons, leaf-eating langurs and pygmy lorises—were just outside the gate. More than 100 animals, confiscated from wildlife traders, hunters, pet owners and a restaurant, live in the airy tree-shaded cages and five acres of semiwild enclosures of the Endangered Primate Rescue Center. Ordinarily viewing primates is like trying to watch a party in a fifth-floor apartment while you're standing outside on the street. But we were at street level at the rescue center as I walked along the paths between cages. In one, two baby gibbons swung on boat-hook arms taking noisy dives at their mother. Without looking up from grooming herself, she'd pluck one from the air and tickle the squealing bundle mercilessly before letting go ... Fifteen different primate species live here, but some of them are likely to disappear soon.

One-fifth of the world's 25 most endangered primates live in Vietnam, and one or more of them will become extinct in the next few decades.

Source: *The New York Times* Sunday 28 July 2002

Variation

You could ask more advanced students to make the code a little more complicated: definite articles in yellow, indefinite articles in purple, countable nouns in pink, non-countable nouns in grey, conjunctions in orange, and so on.

5.6 Let's experiment

Level Lower-elementary and above

Time IN CLASS 10–15 minutes
HOMEWORK 60 minutes

Aims To encourage students to use the target language outside class.

Preparation

Write a letter to each student containing the instructions for their assignment. Some examples are given on the next page.

Dear ______________,

Ask someone in English how he or she feels, what he or she is doing, and what he or she did at the weekend.

Good luck!
From,

Dear ______________,

Ask someone in English what technological or medical advances will be made in the next twenty years, in his or her opinion.

Good luck!
From,

Dear ______________,

Ask someone in English what he or she was doing this time yesterday.

Good luck!
From,

Dear ______________,

Ask someone in English what he or she will have done by the end of the day.

Good luck!
From,

Dear ______________,

Ask someone in English what he or she is planning to do this weekend.

Good luck!
From,

Dear ______________,

Ask someone in English what he or she is planning to do for a holiday.

Good luck!
From,

Dear ______________,

Ask someone in English what he or she usually does at weekends.

Good luck!
From,

Procedure

1 Distribute the letters in class and instruct the students to open and read them once they are at home. Ask students to complete the tasks and then note down where and with whom they used the language. They should find native English speakers or other students to talk to.

2 When the students are back in class, ask them to explain to other students what they talked about for their homework and how they completed their tasks.

Variation 1

Give the students the letters in class, ask them to read them and to practise the appropriate language with a partner for the last few minutes of the lesson. Students should use the target language as naturally as possible—so naturally, in fact, that their partners don't notice what it is. At the end of the activity, ask the students to guess what each other's target language is.

Variation 2

The tasks could be sent by email, if you have email addresses for all of the students.

Variation 3

If there is a conversation club at the school, this activity could be done during that time.

Variation 4

Students could all be given the same target language to use.

5.7 What did you hear?

Level Upper-intermediate and above

Time IN CLASS 10–15 minutes
HOMEWORK 30 minutes +

Aims To encourage grammar practice while using a much-loved medium—television—as the prompt.

Preparation

Choose suitable television programmes for the students to watch. Note the times and channels, and design suitable tasks (or use those given below).

Procedure

1 Hand out a list of time schedules and channels of programmes that the students should watch. Ask them to watch 10–20 minutes of a programme, if possible. Set a specific task for each programme.

Examples

1 Watch the weather forecast on Channel 11 at 7 p.m. What does the forecaster say the weather will be like at the weekend? (Use future tenses.)

2 Watch the cooking channel and note down a recipe for the class. (Use imperatives!)
3 What is the most popular song on MTV at the moment? In your opinion who is the best singer, the best actor, and the funniest comedian? (Use superlatives.)
4 Describe the main story on the news. (Use past narrative tenses.)
5 What happened in *Friends*? (Use past narrative tenses.)

2 Ask the students to answer the questions in complete sentences, using correct grammatical forms. Note that the students can watch the television programme in their first language, but they must answer the questions in English. Ensure that the students know which English-speaking channels are available in their country, for example, BBC World, CNN, or MTV.

3 In the following lesson, ask students to discuss their work in groups, and then collect in the work.

5.8 What's the context?

Level Intermediate and above

Time IN CLASS 15–20 minutes
HOMEWORK 20–25 minutes +

Aims To help students to remember new structures and to raise their awareness of how the language was taught. This should make the structures more memorable.

Preparation

Prepare a list of structures which the students should study for homework.

Procedure

1 At the end of a lesson, ask the students to think about the new target language that has been presented, and the context that was used for the teaching.

2 Dictate or write on the board previously taught language structures, and ask the students for homework to write down the contexts which were used to present the language.

Example If I were you, I'd find a new boyfriend.

A student might say: 'It was presented by the teacher showing pictures of a boy and girl. The teacher told us that they had a problem. The boy was not a good boyfriend. The girl told her friend about their problems and the friend gave the girl advice.'

3 During the next lesson, ask the students to compare their homework in pairs.

Comments

Students can keep repeating this exercise as a homework task.

Variation 1

Ask the students to create new contexts or places that the language might be used. For example, the third conditional could be used by an unhappily married woman.

Examples If I had known then how I would feel now, I would have got married later in life. If I had listened to my mother, I would have got married at 30, not 20.

Variation 2

Dictate structures to the students at the end of class, and ask them to decide who said the sentences and when—i.e. what was the situation.

Examples I wish I'd thought about that before!
I was going to try that but I didn't.
I was really surprised when I saw him.
I am going to go to university next year.

Variation 3

Ask the students to think of one structure and as many different ways it can be used as possible, and say where it is found.

Example The passive can be found in a newspaper, in instructions in a computer manual, in a cake recipe, etc.

5.9 Things I need to remember

Level Pre-intermediate and above

Time IN CLASS 10 minutes +
HOMEWORK 30 minutes +

Aims To make students aware of the vital areas of a new piece of target language.

Preparation

Note down a certain piece of target language, and the areas of difficulty students have with it.

Procedure

1 After presenting the target structure, for example, the present simple, end the lesson by writing a sentence on the board using the structure.
2 Organize the students into pairs and ask them to think of what they need to remember about that structure:

Example **Present simple**

Third person *-s*

Different sounds at the end, i.e. *passes* /iz/ *stops* /s/ *tries* /z/

Used for talking about daily habits

Students will need to be prompted to think of important features, i.e. pronunciation, form, meaning, and use.

3 For homework, ask the students to review this and add another grammatical structure you have taught, for example, the past simple, and to write down the important points they need to remember about it.
4 At the beginning of the next lesson, ask the students to compare their research.

Comments

Younger learners can make a poster or collage out of the special things they need to remember.

Variation

Ask the students specific questions about the grammatical structures that you would like them to research and remember.

Example **Present simple**

1 What is the sound at the end of *stops*?
2 What happens when *he* or *she* is the subject?
3 How do you make the sentence negative?
4 What do you have to add when you make a question?
5 Put these into sentences using *he* or *she*: *try, watch, make*.

5.10 Which error do I make frequently?

Level Pre-intermediate and above

Time IN CLASS 15 + minutes
HOMEWORK 45 minutes +

Aims To make students aware of errors they make repeatedly.

Preparation

Prepare a list of errors which students have made frequently during lessons.

Procedure

1 At the end of a lesson, give the students a list of frequently made errors and ask them, in pairs, to correct them.

2 Discuss the corrections.

Follow-up

Ask the students to monitor their work over the next few weeks to see which errors they make repeatedly. They can do this by noting down the errors which you correct during lessons in the backs of their notebooks. Keep going over the corrections during lessons and ask the students for homework to investigate why these errors are made. Ask them to write down an explanation. For example, they may not have certain structures in their own language, or the lexical items that they mistake may be false friends.

Comments

This activity is very successful with students who are not good at listening to oral corrections in class. They need to see the errors for themselves and to engage cognitively in correcting them. This recognition of frequently made errors is particularly useful for exam students and business students who would like to accelerate their improvement.

5.11 A question I have

Level Pre-intermediate and above

Time IN CLASS 15–20 minutes +
HOMEWORK 30 minutes +

Aims To allow the students to ask questions that they may feel hesitant about asking in class. To create an open dialogue between you and the students on a one-to-one basis, which nervous or shy students may appreciate.

Preparation

Think of possible questions that the students may want to ask about certain grammatical structures.

Procedure

1. At the end of class, organize the students into pairs to discuss any difficulties they are having with certain grammatical structures.
2. Ask the students for homework to write down questions about these grammatical structures.
3. In the next class, collect in the questions and write answers to the students, to be returned with their questions.

Comments

This can help the weaker students, but also helps to clarify points for all students. It will enable you to see your students clearly as individuals, and appreciate their particular needs.

5.12 What's the difference between ...?

Level Intermediate and above

Time IN CLASS 15–20 minutes
HOMEWORK 40–60 minutes +

Aims To encourage students to think clearly about the differences between their own language and English.

Preparation

Note down some differences between English and the students' first language.

Procedure

1. At the end of class, ask the students in pairs to discuss how certain grammatical structures, which they have learnt in English, would be used in their own language.
2. For homework, ask them to write down the differences that they can see between the grammatical structures they have learnt in English and the corresponding structures in their first language.
3. In class, discuss these differences and note down the students' answers. Make sure that this develops into a class discussion and have fun looking at the foibles of English. Allow students to question any differences, and encourage them to keep pointing them out during lessons.
4. Write all of the differences on a worksheet which can be given to present and future learners so that they can avoid making certain mistakes when learning English. A Polish group I had made this worksheet together:

Example

ENGLISH	POLISH
ð sound	*What's this?*
If I do that I will ...	Not *If I will do that I will ...*
I want, he wants	Not: *want ...* (no subject)
Plurals	No plurals
Articles	No articles

Encourage your students to write notes such as the ones above, which can be used as a quick reference. This is useful for exam students.

5.13 Quiz

Level **Intermediate and above**

Time **IN CLASS** **10 minutes**
HOMEWORK **15 minutes +**

Aims **To review various tenses in a fun way and engage students in thinking about the language, as well as using it.**

Preparation

Photocopy a quiz sheet for each student in class.

Procedure

1 At the end of a lesson, hand out a quiz sheet to each student and ask them to complete it at home.

Quiz

1 What is the past tense of *weep*, which rhymes with *swept*?
2 What is the past of *lie*, which looks like (but doesn't sound like) *said*?
3 What sounds like it's in a pencil, and is the past of *lead*?
4 What grammatical structure in the future tense, in a sentence, sounds like *wheel*?
5 Which *need* do you use when you make bread?
6 What *wood* do I need in the second conditional?
7 Can I say informations? Why/why not?
8 What kinds of articles do you find in a news article?

2 Discuss the answers in the following lesson.

Answers

1 wept
2 laid
3 led
4 we'll (we will)
5 knead
6 would
7 No, because it's uncountable
8 definite and indefinite articles

Follow-up

Ask the students to write their own quiz questions; collect them in and then either set them in class or redistribute them for further homework.

5.14 Grammar jazz chants/rhymes

Level Elementary and above

Time IN CLASS 15–20 minutes
HOMEWORK 40 minutes +

Aims To help students to memorize grammar structures as well as to help them to hear rhythm in English.

Preparation

Decide on a jazz chant to use in class (see anything from Carolyn Graham's *Jazz Chant* books).

Procedure

1. After you have taught a particular grammar structure, do a jazz chant with your students. They will probably have fun doing this, as well as feeling that they are pronouncing the structure well. Ask the students why such an activity is useful. Try to elicit from them the fact that it also aids memory.
2. For homework ask the students to write a jazz chant for the structure themselves. If necessary, set specific guidelines, such as a four-line rhyme which practises the past simple. Remind them of the one you did in class.
3. Collect and read the students' chants to see if they work. Correct them and then try some in class. Note that the main aim is not that students create a good chant, but that they try to review the target structure in a particular way.

Variation 1

If a chant appears too ambitious for your class, ask the students to create a little rhyme. Here are some examples written by intermediate students:

Examples *The simple past*

I went to bed and laid down my head,
I fell asleep and didn't say a peep.

Will

I will go out tonight
To watch a fight.

I will try to win some money
Or find something funny.

Variation 2

For lower-level students, especially beginners and elementary students, teach them a rhyme and ask them to memorize it for homework. This is especially fun with younger learners, who can practise rhymes with friends and parents.

6
Focus on communication

'Of all the four skills (listening, speaking, reading and writing), speaking seems intuitively the most important: people who know the language are referred to as "speakers" of the language', wrote Penny Ur in *A Course in Language Teaching.* Very often students want to be able to communicate orally more than they want other skills, and in class we need to spend time developing this. I often feel that this is rehearsal time, a preparation for when students will speak English in a real-life situation. What we do in class is to create situations which are as near to the real thing as possible.

Productive skills rely on the student feeling confident and able to experiment freely without fear of making mistakes. Homework is an excellent opportunity for students to develop their confidence and to experiment, away from the listening teacher and classmates. It allows students valuable assimilation time—things they have learnt in class need to be filtered and made into their own language before they feel comfortable using them. In class, there is usually insufficient time to allow for real acquisition. In *How to be a More Successful Language Learner*, Joan Rubin and Irene Thompson advise students to 'play with the language to develop a feeling for how it works. The language must, in some sense, become part of you rather than remain an external mechanical system that you manipulate.'

In this chapter, a variety of guided tasks aim to help students develop their fluency in English. The activities allow students to 'play' and to experiment. For example, in the first activity, students are given language to use outside class and asked to note down reactions and bring their research back to class. The more students practise, the more they will become familiar with the language in terms of meaning, use and pronunciation.

There aren't many pen-and-paper activities in this chapter; therefore you will need to keep asking students about the tasks and how they felt doing them in order to create an open dialogue about their usefulness. Where students recognize the value of the tasks they should be motivated to continue with them. They will develop learner autonomy and start to do the tasks without your prompting. The aim is that as a teacher you set up frameworks for tasks and the students, once they have tried something successfully, keep repeating it and begin to expand their own learning independently. The language content for each task can be changed as the learner progresses in his or her studies.

Organizing outside trips

One of the most important parts of learning English is to expand from the classroom into the outside world. Trips are always a favourite with students—they are memorable, fun, and provide excellent directed exposure to English and/or opportunities to use English. If you are in a non-English speaking country, the students can use English when showing others around their town. The activities in the latter part of this chapter help to structure outside trips. Some involve you as a teacher, which means that they should be done during class time and therefore are not strictly homework activities. Most, however, can be done by the students independently.

6.1 Structured conversation

Level Beginner/elementary and above

Time IN CLASS 15 minutes +
HOMEWORK 45 minutes +

Aims To provide practice of language taught in class. To encourage the students to 'play' with the language and record the results of their efforts.

Preparation

Write a list of questions using the target language from class, and photocopy the questions for your students.

Procedure

1 Give each student a list of questions, and instruct them to use the questions with either native speakers of English or other students of English outside class.

Example **Questions which review the past continuous and simple past**

1 What did you do last night?
2 What were you doing at 7 p.m. last night?
3 What was your first job?
4 Where did you go on your last vacation?
5 What did you do last weekend?
6 What were you doing at 10 a.m. yesterday?
7 What were you doing when you heard about Princess Diana's accident?

2 Students should note down the answers they receive when they ask the questions, and bring them into class. During the next lesson, ask the students to compare the answers they received.

Comments

This is a particularly useful activity for business students who are concerned with how their English sounds and with their accuracy. Beginners will obviously be limited by how much they can ask, but they can ask two or three questions they have learnt from class.

Variation 1

Provide higher-level students with discussion questions, instead of questions that practise a particular grammatical structure. Explain that they should discuss the questions with as many people as possible and should bring the answers they receive back to class.

Discussion questions

Is it possible to have a just war?
Do you think that cloning will be a normal occurrence in the future?
Are rainforests doomed?
Do you believe in love at first sight?

Variation 2

Students can tape the questions and answers. Ask students to listen to the recordings, note down the answers, and say what improvements they would make to their own English. The students could also write their own questions for a native or near-native speaker to answer on tape. Check the students' questions first and correct them, if necessary. Collect in their tapes and listen to the students' work, providing written feedback for them.

6.2 Real life

Level Elementary and above

Time IN CLASS 10–15 minutes
HOMEWORK 40–60 minutes +

Aims To encourage students to practise functional language outside class and to complete real-life tasks which will make homework meaningful.

Preparation

Design a task or tasks you would like the students to do (see examples below).

Procedure

1 Prepare the students by reviewing the functional language they will need for their tasks.

2 Give the students the task(s) and a deadline for completion. In non-English-speaking countries, the students should translate the information they find into English and present it to the class.

Examples

1 Find out the train times to ______ (a town/city near you).
2 Find out the range of ticket prices for the local subway/metro/buses.
3 Choose a tourist destination nearby and find out how to get there.
4 Find out where you can use the Internet near your place of learning.
5 Go to a chemist's and ask how much a bottle of shampoo costs. Ask the shopkeeper to recommend a shampoo for your hair and ask how much the conditioner costs.

6 Go to a local shop. Ask the shopkeeper his or her name, ask for the time, ask when the shop closes, when it opens and when are the busiest days.
7 Find out how you join the public library.
8 Find out where you can go swimming and how much it costs.
9 Go to the post office and find out how much it costs to send a letter to ______ (choose destination).
10 Find out where you can buy a newspaper in English.
11 What information does the local tourist office have in English? Pick up one leaflet about an important landmark and ask the tourist guide about it in English.
12 Find out which channels are in English on the television.

3 In the next lesson, ask each student to tell the rest of the group about the task he or she completed and the information obtained.

Variation

Lower-level students could try the tasks below:

1 Find out how much a loaf of bread costs.
2 Find out where the nearest bank is.
3 Find out where you can buy eggs, cheese, and cold meats.
4 Ask someone how to get to the post office.
5 Ask for directions to the nearest library.

You may need to translate the instructions into their first language. Ask them to note down the answers in their own language, but to translate them into English for the class.

6.3 Beginner review

Level Beginner and above

Time IN CLASS 10 minutes
HOMEWORK 10–15 minutes per session

Aims To help beginner students to develop their confidence, especially in their ability to remember words and use them correctly.

Materials Picture of objects (or the objects themselves) from the lexical set you are teaching.

Procedure

1 When you have taught certain lexical sets in class, for example, foods, furniture, rooms, and so on, ask the students to do an appropriate task like the ones listed below.

Examples

1 Go to the grocer's with a friend and name the fruit and vegetables in English.
2 Go to the chemist's with a friend and name some of the products in English.
3 Go to the supermarket with a friend and name some of the products in English.
4 Name the rooms in your house/apartment in English.

5 Name the foods in your fridge in English. Make English labels for them if possible.
6 Name the things in your bedroom/living room in English.

You may need to translate the instructions into the students' first language, or you can demonstrate the activity by showing students a picture of a shop or room and naming the objects in class.

2 In class, show students some objects (or pictures of objects) that they may have seen. As you hold them up in class, prompt the students to say the name.

3 Ask them to use these words in sentences.

6.4 Using cue cards

Level Beginner and above

Time IN CLASS 10–15 minutes
HOMEWORK 20–45 minutes

Aims To encourage new learners to practise class-taught language orally in a way which will help them to memorize target language as well as develop accurate use of the language.

Preparation

Photocopy a cue card for each student.

Procedure

1 Give each student a verb cue card like the ones opposite and ask them to use the cues in order to repeat a particular language structure that has been taught in class.

2 Ask the students, for homework, to use the cues to generate sentences.

Example The cue GO could generate 'I went home last night' (as a review of the simple past). The cue GET UP could generate 'I get up at 8 a.m.' (as a review of the simple present).

Remind the students that this is oral practice, not written practice.

3 When the students are back in class, ask them to share their sentences and practise them with the rest of the group. They can do this in groups of four; one student should hold up a cue card, say an appropriate sentence, and ask the other students to repeat it.

Go

Get up

Work

Write

Eat

Drink

Meet

Visit

6.5 Telephone calls

Level Pre-intermediate and above

Time IN CLASS 10–15 minutes
HOMEWORK 2–3 minutes per call

Aims To help students gain confidence speaking on the telephone.

Preparation

Collect the students' telephone numbers and organize a time when you can call them. This will be time-consuming for you, so organize the activity over several weeks and call one or two students per week.

Procedure

1 In class, explain that you are going to telephone the students and speak to them for a few minutes.
2 Make the calls and ask students a set question, for example, what they did at work, what they did during the day, what they have been studying.
3 Next lesson, ask the students to discuss what they talked about on the phone in pairs.

Comments

It is best to do this with groups you know very well, so that they will feel at ease speaking on the phone rather than have long nervous pauses.

Variation 1

Give certain information over the telephone which the students should note down, for example, a recipe with instructions, or dates and times for events.

Variation 2

If students are in an English-speaking country, provide them with telephone numbers for the local cinema listing, tourist information, bus information, and so on, and set specific information-gathering tasks.

Examples

1 Call the cinema; the number is ________ .
Find out if the movie ________ is showing.

2 Call the train station; the number is ________ .
Find out what time the train to ________ leaves tonight.

3 Call the theatre; the number is ________ .
Find out how much a ticket to see a musical costs.

Variation 3

Lower-level students can also do this task, but they may need to have the instructions translated for them, and only one or two questions should be asked over the phone, such as 'How are you?' 'What did you do today?'

6.6 Telephone whispers

Level Pre-intermediate and above

Time IN CLASS 10–15 minutes
HOMEWORK 1–2 minutes per call

Aims To encourage students to speak in English on the telephone, and to improve their listening skills along with their speaking skills.

Preparation

Collect the students' telephone numbers and make a list to give to the class.

Procedure

1 This activity is the same as the game of Chinese whispers, but is played over the telephone.
2 Start by demonstrating the game in class with the students. Arrange the students in a line (one student behind the other). Whisper a sentence in the ear of the first student, who should then pass it to the next student by whispering it in his or her ear. This is continued to the last person in the line, who says the sentence out loud. Usually it is not quite the same as the original sentence!
3 Explain the homework version to students: you will telephone the first student on the list and say a sentence to him or her. The student then has to call the next person on the telephone list and repeat it. If a student is unable to reach the next student on the list, he or she should call the following one.
4 The final person on the list should write down the sentence and bring it to class.

Comments

This is good fun but does need to be arranged carefully, with specific times and days. My experience has been that students find this very motivating as a homework task.

6.7 Night-time questions

Level Beginner and above

Time IN CLASS 15–20 minutes (optional)
HOMEWORK 30–45 minutes

Aims To encourage students to review language at any time of the day and to help them to memorize language, developing both fluency and accuracy.

Preparation

Photocopy the list of questions on the next page, or prepare your own questions.

Procedure

1 Give each student a copy of the 'night-time questions' below or your own questions. Ask them to consider these questions just before they go to bed. They should answer them in their heads or out loud. If the students need preparation, ask them to answer the questions in class first, and then answer them again at home.

> **Night-time questions**
>
> 1 What did you do today?
> 2 What was the best thing that you did today?
> 3 What made you smile/laugh today?
> 4 What did you watch on television?
> 5 Who did you speak to on the telephone?
> 6 What did you see/hear on the news?

2 Ask the students to think about the structures and lexical items they use when answering the questions, so that they are aware of the language. They should try to remember any corrections you made when they were speaking in class.

3 Ask them also to think of other questions they would like to ask the students in class.

4 Next lesson, ask the students to comment on what they found out.

Comments

Some students who did this activity said that speaking in front of a mirror helped; it's worth a try!

Variation

Lower-level students could answer these questions:

> **Questions**
>
> 1 How are you?
> 2 What do you do?
> 3 Where do you come from?
> 4 What do you like to do in your free time?
> 5 What do you usually do at the weekends?

6.8 Taped journal

Level Pre-intermediate and above

Time IN CLASS 10–20 minutes
HOMEWORK 5–15 minutes per session

Aims To encourage students to practise talking about a variety of subjects which are relevant to them. Also to encourage them to listen to themselves while speaking, so they can focus on their own accuracy along with fluency.

Preparation

Photocopy the questions on page 97 for each student, and the journal entries if required.

Sunday March 28th

I got up late. My head was throbbing from the terrible music at the party the night before. I saw Jenny and John together having fun. He loves her I suppose—not me!

He looked very nice in his new sweater. I noticed that he was wearing the jacket I bought him. Do you think I should ask for it back? Or should I just throw wine all over it by accident?
Diary, tell me time heals!

Monday March 29th

Saw John get on to the bus. He still lives in his old flat I suppose—and I still have the key to that flat, Diary! I plan to make a visit!

Tuesday March 30th

Diary, I made the mistake of my life. I went to the flat and wanted to speak to John but SHE was there. Oh Diary, why didn't I listen to you!

Procedure

1 Introduce the idea of a journal in class by showing students an example. Use the one on page 96 if appropriate, and ask the students what is happening in this journal. Who do they think wrote it, and why did the person write this? (To confide in the diary as if it were a person.)

Ask the students to think about the kind of things that people write in journals or diaries, such as the day's events, daily routine, etc. Note these on the board. This will prompt students in the following stage.

2 Organize students into pairs and have them ask each other the question in the box below.

> **Journal questions**
>
> 1 What do you usually do in your free time?
> 2 What did you do yesterday?
> 3 What did you eat?
> 4 How did you feel at the end of the day?
> 5 Did something unusual happen to you?

3 Ask the students to start an English journal at home, recorded on tape. The students can use the above questions as prompts as to what to say.

Comments

The students do not have to let you or anyone else listen to their tapes—they are personal. One important benefit of doing this is that the students will be able to monitor their own oral progress.

Variation

Business students or one-to-one students could record an account of their daily experiences, for you to correct in class.

6.9 Tape as a monitor

Level Beginner and above

Time IN CLASS 15–20 minutes (optional)
HOMEWORK 20–30 minutes per session

Aims To encourage students to listen to themselves speaking English. This will not only develop their listening skills, but will also develop accuracy as they become aware of how they sound in English.

Materials

Tape and a tape machine if desired.

Procedure

1 If you wish, introduce the idea by taping the students doing an activity in class; play back the tape to the students so they can have fun listening to themselves (possibly they will not have done this before).

2 Ask the students to record themselves speaking in English for homework.

Example
- describing themselves
- talking about a subject they are interested in
- explaining how to use something, such as a cash machine
- talking about the family.

3 Ask the students to keep recording themselves over the months, whenever they have free time.

4 Keep providing the students with talking points, such as questions about a topic covered in class, or questions that require the target language from lessons. For example, if health was covered in class, ask the students to discuss whether they think they are particularly healthy, or what they do in order to stay healthy. If you have recently taught the past continuous, ask: 'What were you doing at 7 p.m. yesterday?' At the end of a course, the students should have taped themselves several times.

Comments

Students can then monitor and assess their own progress, for example, using the worksheet below and giving themselves scores or writing comments. If they do this from the beginning of their course, they should be able to see their progress and therefore feel motivated to continue their studies.

	Tape 1 Date:	**Tape 2** Date:	**Tape 3** Date:	**Tape 4** Date:
Vocabulary				
Grammar				
Pronunciation				
Fluency				

Variation

If you have smaller groups, such as a business group, encourage them to bring their tapes into class and give feedback about their English. They will probably know what they would like to record, such as a business presentation, and you can encourage them to be self-directed.

6.10 Describe the picture

Level Pre-intermediate and above

Time IN CLASS 20–30 minutes
HOMEWORK 45 minutes +

Aims To encourage students to prepare for oral presentations in class. This will allow students to consider the language that they want to use in class, making them more confident.

Preparation

Collect postcards, cut out pictures from magazines, or photocopy the pictures on page 100 (one for each student).

Procedure

1 Give a picture to each student and dictate the questions below. Ask them to use the picture as a prompt and work on these questions at home in preparation for an oral presentation in class.

2 In the next class, organize the students into pairs and ask them to answer questions like Worksheet A orally for their partners.

Worksheet A

1 What has happened?
2 What is going to happen?
3 Who do you think the people are in the picture?
4 What is the atmosphere like?
5 Where was the picture taken?

Variation

For lower-level students, use pictures of people. Set them questions like Worksheet B for homework. Tell the students to use their imaginations when writing the answers. In the next lesson they should present information about their fictitious people to the class.

6.10

POLICE
POLIC
POLIC
CROSS
DO NOT CR
POLICE . DO NOT
POLICE. DO NOT CROS

Worksheet B

1 What does he or she do?
2 What is his or her name?
3 Where is he or she from?
4 What does he or she like to do in his or her free time?
5 How old is he or she?
6 How big is his or her family?

6.11 The art gallery

Level **Elementary and above**

Time IN CLASS **10–15 minutes. For the high-level activity, you may need to pre-teach some of the lexical items; this could take up to 40 minutes**

HOMEWORK **60–80 minutes**

Aims **To exploit an interest students may have in art and to use visual stimuli from outside class, which adds variety and enriches the students' learning experience.**

Preparation

Visit the local art gallery and find out what type of work is on display. Note down information which can be used to make a questionnaire about the artwork or the gallery itself, or use the worksheets supplied. Worksheet A is for lower-level students, and Worksheet B for higher levels. With the higher-level worksheet, either pre-teach the words in the task or explain to the students that they will need to use a dictionary to do the task.

Procedure

1 At the end of a class, ask the students to tell you where the art gallery is in town. Ask them if they have been there and whether they enjoy going. Tell them that it is going to be their classroom for the next homework task.

2 Hand out your questionnaire about the art gallery and ask the students to go to the gallery and find the information for you in English. If you use the higher-level worksheet, make sure that the students understand the vocabulary.

Worksheet A

1 What times is the gallery open?
2 How much does it cost to get in?
3 How can I get there?
4 What is the gallery near?
5 Describe a painting that you like.
6 Name two or three of the artists in the gallery.

Worksheet B

1 Choose a picture that makes you happy. Describe it. Try to use some of the words below to explain the colours used in the picture and the picture itself.

Colours	**Texture**	**Feeling/ mood**	**Picture type**
Rich	Smooth	Sunny	Abstract
Pale	Grainy	Joyful	Cubist
Pastel	Silky	Humorous	Oil painting
Vibrant	Rough	Sentimental	Watercolour
Dazzling	Shiny	Religious	Impressionist
Vivid	Coarse	Optimistic	Old master
Dull	Textured	Light-hearted	Surreal
Bright	Delicate	Serious	Modern

2 Explain why the picture makes you happy.
3 Choose a picture that makes you feel depressed.
4 Why does it upset you?
5 Find a picture which makes you feel confused, frustrated, or puzzled.
6 Why does it make you feel this way?
7 Is there a picture which is breathtaking?

3 In the next lesson, ask the students to tell their partners what they found and saw.
4 Collect in the students' written work and correct it.

Variation

1 Draw the rectangle below on the board at the end of a class. Ask the students to copy it in their notebooks. Ask them to visit an art gallery and to choose a picture to describe, using the rectangle as a prompt.
2 In the following lesson, let the students describe their pictures either to the whole group, or in pairs.

There is a bird in the upper left-hand corner which is flying across the sky.		There is a big sun in the upper right-hand corner. It is shining brightly.
	In the foreground there is a man fishing.	
In the lower left-hand corner there is a dog. The dog is barking.		In the lower right-hand corner there is a woman She is sleeping.

Follow-up

Bring in pictures and ask the students to describe them, either in pairs if you have a large class, or as a whole group activity.

6.12 A museum visit

Level Elementary and above

Time IN CLASS 60 minutes
HOMEWORK 60 minutes +

Aims To encourage students to use the resources around them, i.e. museums and art galleries. Also to encourage the students to activate their English outside class as much as possible.

Materials

Brochures/leaflets from a local museum.

Procedure

1 Bring into class some brochures from the nearest museum. Tell the students how to get there and explain that their homework involves visiting the museum.

2 Ask the students to go to the museum and find an artefact that they really like. Tell them to ask a museum guide for information about the artefact and to write a mini-presentation for class about it. They can speak in English if the guide speaks English, or use their first language if necessary, but they must write notes in English.

3 In the next lesson, collect in the notes for the presentations and correct them.

4 Allow time in class for the students to give their presentations.

Comments

Younger learners can draw the object and display their work in class.

6.13 Being a guide

Level All

Time IN CLASS 10–15 minutes
HOMEWORK 60–80 minutes

Aims To provide students with realistic applications of functional English.

Preparation

Decide on locations for the students to visit and compile a questionnaire for them to complete (see examples on pages 105–6). Alternatively, ask the students to suggest a place they would like to visit and create a questionnaire they can complete while visiting.

Procedure

1 Ask the students, in pairs or with an English-speaking friend, to visit the places you suggest (provide addresses) and to answer the questions on the worksheets in English. They should speak in English as much as possible on their visit.

2 Ask students to note down the things they discussed so that they can present them in class.

At the pharmacy

Discuss the questions below with your friend in English.
Ask someone, if you don't know all of the answers.
Note down your answers.

1. Find a painkiller, show your friend the packet and explain the instructions for taking it.
2. What can you take if you have a sore throat?
3. Can you buy toothpaste in the shop? Show your friend the brand you use and explain why you like it.
4. Where can you collect prescriptions?
5. What can you take for indigestion? How much should you take per day? Explain to your friend.

At the bank

Discuss the questions below with your friend in English.
Ask someone, if you don't know all of the answers.
Note down your answers.

1. Explain to your friend how you deposit money in the bank.
2. Explain to your friend how you withdraw money.
3. Explain how you buy traveller's cheques.
4. Explain how you obtain a loan from the bank; ask a teller and then explain to your friend in English.
5. Tell your friend what other services the bank offers.

At the post office

Discuss the questions below with your friend in English.
Ask someone, if you don't know all of the answers.
Note down your answers.

1. Tell your friend how to buy stamps at the post office.
2. Tell your friend what you have to do if you want to send a parcel overseas.
3. Describe one service you use in the post office.
4. Ask your friend what he or she uses the post office for.

At the grocery store

Discuss the questions below with your friend in English.
Ask someone, if you don't know all of the answers.
Note down your answers.

1 Show your friend the vegetables and fruit and name them for him or her.
2 Find out how much a kilo of tomatoes and a kilo of potatoes cost, and tell your friend.
3 Tell your friend which are your favourite vegetables.
4 Tell your friend which is your favourite fruit.
5 Ask your friend which are his or her favourite fruit and vegetables.

6.14 We're going to the zoo

Level Pre-intermediate and above

Time IN CLASS 10–15 minutes
HOMEWORK 60–80 minutes

Aims To encourage the students to match an outside interest with the use of English.

Preparation

Visit the local zoo or wildlife park, see what animals are there, and the type of information that can be found in English. Photocopy the worksheets on page 107, one for each student in the group. Worksheet A is for higher-level students, and Worksheet B for lower levels.

Procedure

1 Ask the students, at the end of class, where the zoo or wildlife park is. Ask them if they have been there.
2 Hand out the questionnaire to each student.
3 Ask them to take a partner from class or an English-speaking friend to the zoo and to answer the questions.
4 Next lesson, ask the students to discuss their answers.

Worksheet A

1 Tell your friend which is your favourite animal and ask which is his or hers.
2 Find a mammal in the zoo and tell your friend about it.
3 Find out what is special about reptiles. Name three types in the zoo.
4 Find an animal which eats only fruit and vegetables.
5 Find a carnivore in the zoo.
6 Find a nocturnal animal.
7 Find an animal that is a predator.
8 Discuss this question with your friend: Are zoos a good thing or a bad thing?

Worksheet B

1 Name three animals that you like, and show them to your friend.
2 Choose one animal and answer these questions with your friend:
   a What type of animal is it?
   b What does it eat?
   c Does it sleep at night or during the day?
   d Where does it come from?
3 Name three animals that you don't like. Say why don't you like them.

6.15 Create a role

Level Pre-intermediate and above

Time IN CLASS 40–50 minutes
HOMEWORK 20–30 minutes +

Aims To give students the opportunity to create roles for themselves and their classmates.

Preparation

Photocopy the role cards on the next page for each student.

6.16

Name
Age
Nationality
Occupation
Hobbies
Favourite food
Best achievement
Worst mistake
Favourite holiday destination

Procedure

1 At the end of a role play in class, ask the students to think of the necessary ingredients for a good role play, for example, one that is funny, motivating, has interesting roles, and is easy to remember.

2 Tell them that for their next role play in class they are going to create their own roles.

3 Give the students the role cards, and ask them to write in the information at home. Tell them to be creative and to return to class with a completely imagined role.

4 Tell the students that the role play will have a party setting, and that all they will need to do is to act their roles and meet all the other students at the party.

5 In the following lesson, the students should complete the role play by mingling as they act out their roles.

Variation 1

For lower-level students, ask them to write only: name, hobbies, nationality, age, and favourite food (or favourite singer or movie star).

Variation 2

The students could write a role for another member of their class rather than for themselves. Collect the role ideas from the students, check the language that has been used, and then redistribute the roles to different students.

Variation 3

Give the students pictures of people cut out from magazines. Ask them to decide who this is and some facts about the person. When the students come back into class, they can pretend to be that person.

6.16 Cultural differences

Level Intermediate and above

Time IN CLASS 20 minutes +
HOMEWORK 60 minutes +

Aims To expose the students to other cultures and to increase their understanding of how far-reaching English is.

Procedure

1 If the students are studying away from home, ask them to think of the most surprising differences between their native country and their new country. Examples of this could be the food, the washing arrangements, the sleeping arrangements, and so on. Ask the students to think about this for homework, to write a few paragraphs about their thoughts, and be prepared to talk about them.

2 In the next lesson, ask students in pairs to talk about the cultural differences they have noted. Alternatively, ask them to give presentations.

Variation 1

If the students are not living away from home, they may want to consider a place they have visited on holiday and discuss the differences they became aware of.

Variation 2

The students could use movies as a research aid for looking at another culture. For example, when they watch an English-speaking movie they could look for cultural differences—what do the people eat? What do the people wear? What sort of homes do they live in?

Comments

This is usually a good talking topic, and something that can motivate all students. For example, a Brazilian student couldn't believe the new fashions in New York and prepared a whole series of talks about fashion in the US compared with fashion in Brazil. A Japanese student watched a Brazilian movie called *Central Station* and gave a presentation on the differences between Brazil's and Japan's train stations.

7
Focus on pronunciation

Consider how students can help themselves with pronunciation. It is usually an area where they feel they need to have the teacher present in order to model pronunciation and correct them. However, in a classroom it is hard to help students to improve their pronunciation—you need to listen to each individual systematically and help on a one-to-basis, which is sometimes impractical in larger classes. Even in smaller classes, such attention to detail can lead to the pace of the lesson becoming dangerously slow.

Consider these questions:

1 How best do you perfect your own pronunciation of a foreign language?
2 Do you feel self-conscious when speaking in class in front of others?
3 What do your particular group of students need to work on?

Judy Gilbert writes in *ELT News*: 'In an ideal English curriculum, all students would have a class dedicated to pronunciation/listening comprehension. They would get systematic instruction and adequate practice in the most useful concepts and they would learn how all of these concepts are interrelated through the rhythm and melody of the spoken language. So much for the ideal. In real life, teachers typically have to squeeze pronunciation into their class work by sheer cunning. And because time is so limited, rather severe decisions have to be made about what's really important, leaving everything else for some later time.'

Work you would like to do in class can be done at home. This chapter shows that, through homework, you can direct the students towards exercises which focus them on what they need to work on. Obvious tools for this are the phonemic alphabet and listening activities. At home, students can help themselves and work at their own pace.

7.1 Collect a *schwa*

Level Intermediate and above

Time IN CLASS 10–20 minutes
HOMEWORK 30 minutes +

Aims **To raise students' awareness of the frequency of the *schwa* sound. Hearing the *schwa* will lead to the students becoming aware of the connectedness of speech.**

Preparation

Prepare materials which include the *schwa* sound, for example, a tongue twister or a tape script in which the *schwa* can be heard.

Procedure

1 Familiarize the students with the *schwa* by modelling the sound and using your chosen materials which contain it.

Example Homework is **a** useful thing to do.

2 Once the students can recognize the *schwa*, ask them to listen for the sound for homework. They can listen for the sound in the street if they are in an English-speaking country, listen in a song, or listen as they are watching a movie or the television. They should note down sentences or words they have heard which contain the *schwa* sound.

3 In class, remind the students of the sound and ask how many times they heard the sound when they were listening outside class.

Variation

With advanced students, show them part of a movie/video while they follow copies of the script. Ask the students to try to recognize the *schwa* and mark it on the script as they are watching. This procedure can be done with other individual sounds. With lower-level students, play a piece of listening material from their course books and ask the students to follow the tape script. Point out the *schwa* sound as the students listen. Follow this by drilling the students with a few sentences which contain the sound.

7.2 What is different?

Level Intermediate and above

Time IN CLASS 10–15 minutes
HOMEWORK 30 minutes +

Aims **To make students aware of differences between English sounds and the sounds of their first language. This will help students to recognize areas which may potentially be difficult.**

Procedure

1. At the end of a lesson, present the students with an English sound which does not occur in the students' first language. For example, the /ð/ or /θ/ sounds, do not occur in Polish.
2. Ask the students to brainstorm words in English which contain that sound.
3. For homework, set the students the task of finding another sound that occurs in English, but not in their own language. They can do this by watching television, using their dictionaries, listening to the radio, or by talking to an English speaker.
4. Once back in class, students should compare their findings. They can make a poster display showing words which contain the sounds. This will act as a constant reminder.

Variation

With elementary students, give them words which contain a new sound on pieces of card. Ask them to practise saying the sound for homework. Write the words on a poster which can be displayed in the classroom to remind the students of the difference between English and their first language.

Example For Polish students:

THE THEN THAT THIS THOSE THINK

7. 3 Writing tongue twisters

Level Pre-intermediate and above

Time IN CLASS 15–20 minutes
HOMEWORK 40–45 minutes

Aims To encourage students to practise problematical English sounds in a fun way.

Preparation

Select a tongue twister which highlights a particularly problematic sound for the students.

Procedure

1. At the end of a lesson, recite your tongue twister and ask students to repeat it. For example, Polish students could try:

   Thirty-three thirsty theatre-goers thought about the weather. They thought and thought and although they tried hard they couldn't stop the thunder and rain.

2. For homework, ask the students to identify sounds they have difficulty with. Tell them to write their own tongue twisters which contain the sound.
3. When back in class, ask each student to teach his or her tongue twister to the group and to practise saying it.

Variation 1

Students can write jazz chants or rhymes instead of tongue twisters.

Variation 2

Give lower-level students one sentence which contains a sound or sounds with which the students are having difficulty. Model the sentence with the students and then ask them to practise saying the sentence at home.

Example Red roses really are lovely.

If the students know other language learners or native speakers, they could ask them to listen as they say the sentences and to check whether their pronunciation is correct.

7.4 Phonemes

Level All

Time IN CLASS 10 minutes per session
HOMEWORK 30 minutes +

Aims **To introduce the phonemic alphabet to students over a period of time. To help them to see how it will develop their autonomy as learners by becoming an invaluable resource.**

Materials

Cards showing the same phoneme—one copy for each student.

Procedure

1 At the end of a lesson, hand the cards to the students. Ask them to think of a word which begins with this phoneme.

2 Brainstorm words and ask the students to write down some of these words on the backs of their cards.

3 Ask the students to keep the cards near them in the time between lessons. Whenever they have a free moment, for example, on the bus or queuing in the supermarket, they should review the sound and the words. Ask them to mouth the sound to themselves and consider how it is made.

4 When the students are back in class, ask for their words so that they demonstrate the sound for you. Make sure they are making the sound correctly.

Comments

Keep repeating this task. Cover as many useful phonemes as you can over the time you have with the students.

Variation

To extend this activity in class, organize the students into groups of threes or fours. Ask one student from each group to come to the front of the class and look at the phoneme you show them. They should return to the group and make the sound of that phoneme. The group should call out a word which contains the sound. Score a point for the group which calls out a correct word first.

7.5 Transcribing sentences into phonemic script

Level Elementary and above

Time IN CLASS 10–15 minutes
HOMEWORK 45 minutes

Aims To highlight connected speech, an area with which students usually experience problems as soon as they leave class.

Materials

Cards showing phonemically transcribed words.

Preparation

Prepare sentences which the students can transcribe at home.

Procedure

1. As a warm-up, give each student a card with a phonemically transcribed word on it—one that has previously been taught in class. Ask the students to mingle and challenge other students to pronounce the word.
2. At the end of the activity, go over the words and then provide the students with complete sentences using these words.

Example the of a an been have to was

Sentences

- I saw **the** movie on TV last night. It **was** great.
- I'd like **to have a** cup of tea and **an** apple.
- I've **been to** London many times.
- I should **have** done my homework yesterday.

3. Ask the students what connected speech is. Elicit from them the fact that sounds run together and English falls into a rhythm.
4. Repeat the sentences you have given, so that the students are aware of the sounds.
5. For homework ask the students to practise saying the sentences. Ask them to think about what happens to the sounds in connected speech.

Variation

Advanced-level groups could try to transcribe marker sentences (target language in connected speech) from lessons. This will reinforce the pronunciation taught in class and draw students' attention to connected speech.

7.6 Find words with the same sound

Level Pre-intermediate and above

Time IN CLASS 10–15 minutes
HOMEWORK 40–50 minutes

Aims To make students aware of the difference between spelling and the way words are pronounced. This will reinforce the need to be vigilant but also use of the phonemic alphabet.

Preparation

Prepare a list of sounds the students should look for; target sounds with which students are having difficulty.

Procedure

1 At the end of a lesson, give the students a list of individual phonemes and examples of words which contain the sounds.

Examples

/f/	/tʃ/	/θ/
cough	church	theatre
tough	choice	thought
puff	chore	think
stuff	cheese	thought

2 Ask the students for homework to find between ten and twenty words with that sound, either by watching the television in English, looking at a dictionary, or looking at their course books. The students should bring their words into class and read out their lists.

Comments

This is useful for exam students who need to check their pronunciation, but it is equally useful for students who are having problems with their spelling.

Variation

This task can be adapted into a competition, so that students collect as many words as they can and points are scored for correct words.

7.7 Write your own minimal pair list

Level Intermediate and above

Time IN CLASS 10–15 minutes
HOMEWORK 40–50 minutes

Aims To encourage students to concentrate on sounds they find particularly difficult.

Preparation

Copy a list of minimal pairs which highlights sounds with which students are having difficulty.

Procedure

1 Give students the list of minimal pairs. Read out one word in each pair and ask the students to circle the word they hear.

Examples

sheep	cheap
shop	chop
chair	share
bear	pear
post	boast
bow	plough
rain	lane
red	led
road	load

2 Discuss the answers and ask students to brainstorm why this activity is useful.

3 Ask the students, for homework, to write a list of minimal pairs. They should consider the pronunciation work you have done with them and any sounds they are aware of that cause them difficulty.

4 During the next class, collect the lists and keep them for planning future activities, such as dictation activities or listening discrimination activities.

Comments

By asking the students to make up their own lists you will also encourage them to actively consider the sounds of various words.

7.8 Marking stress in individual words

Level Beginner and above

Time IN CLASS 10–20 minutes
HOMEWORK 30–40 minutes

Aims To make students aware of varying word stress. Because the students are advised to use a dictionary, they will also learn another benefit of dictionaries.

Preparation

Decide on a list of recently taught lexical items for the students to concentrate on.

Procedure

1 At the end of a class, review a list of lexical items which have recently been taught. Note them on the board and ask students to pronounce them. Discuss the appropriate stress for the words.

2 Dictate a new list of lexical items and ask the students to mark the stresses over the words for homework; they should use a dictionary to help them.

3 In the next lesson, ask the students to go over their answers and compare them.

Comments

Ask students to continue practising this for all new lexical items.

Variation

This activity can also be done with intonation patterns, or marking problematic sounds.

7.9 Collect patterns

Level Beginner and above

Time IN CLASS 10–15 minutes
HOMEWORK 30–40 minutes

Aims To heighten students' awareness of varying word stress. Also, to emphasize the value of dictionaries for learning outside class.

Preparation

Prepare a list of word-stress patterns for each student using lexical items you have recently taught.

Procedure

1 Give each student a list of varying word stress patterns.

Example

1st syllable stressed	2nd syllable stressed	1st & 3rd syllable stressed
ready	replace	recognize

2 Ask the students for homework to match words they have been taught in class to the stress patterns given. If the students are unsure of the stress patterns, they should check their words in a dictionary.

7.10 Direct a partner

Level Intermediate and above

Time IN CLASS 10–15 minutes
HOMEWORK 45 minutes +

Aims To practise varying intonation patterns and heighten students' awareness of the need to use intonation to express emotions.

Preparation

Prepare a dialogue like the one below.

Procedure

1 Ask the students to imagine a scenario like the following: a robber is in a bank, demanding money from the teller. The teller is quite hard of hearing and cannot really hear the robber through the glass.

Robber:	Put all the money you have into the bag!
Teller:	Put all the what into the bag?
Robber:	Put all the MONEY into the bag!
Teller:	Put all of my money into the back?
Robber:	No, put the money into the BAG!
Teller:	Where should I put it?
Robber:	Into the BAG!
Teller:	Now, where should I put the bag?
Robber:	Give it to me!
Teller:	I'm sorry, I don't think I can do that.

2 Organize the students into groups of three, and give them copies of the dialogue. One student should direct the other two students to act out the dialogue, with the correct stress and real feeling.

3 For homework, ask the students to review the dialogue and then write their own dialogue which could be acted out. The sentences should show similar shifting stress.

Acknowledgement

I got the idea of having students direct each other from *Act English* by Peter Watcyn-Jones.

7.11 Picture sounds

Level Beginner

Time IN CLASS 15 minutes
HOMEWORK 25–45 minutes

Aims **To focus on particularly problematical sounds. The pictures will also help more visual learners to remember the sounds.**

Preparation

Photocopy a picture for each student in class, showing objects whose names contain problematical sounds. Use the pictures overleaf if appropriate.

Procedure

1 At the end of a lesson, give the students a picture each and ask them for homework to label the things in the pictures. Tell students the sound they will be practising in the activity.

2 When back in class, discuss the words they have found and then put these words into sentences. Ask students to practise pronouncing the sentences.

Example *There is a chair next to the table. There is a jug on the table.*
This practises the sounds /dj/ and /tʃ/, and also prepositions.

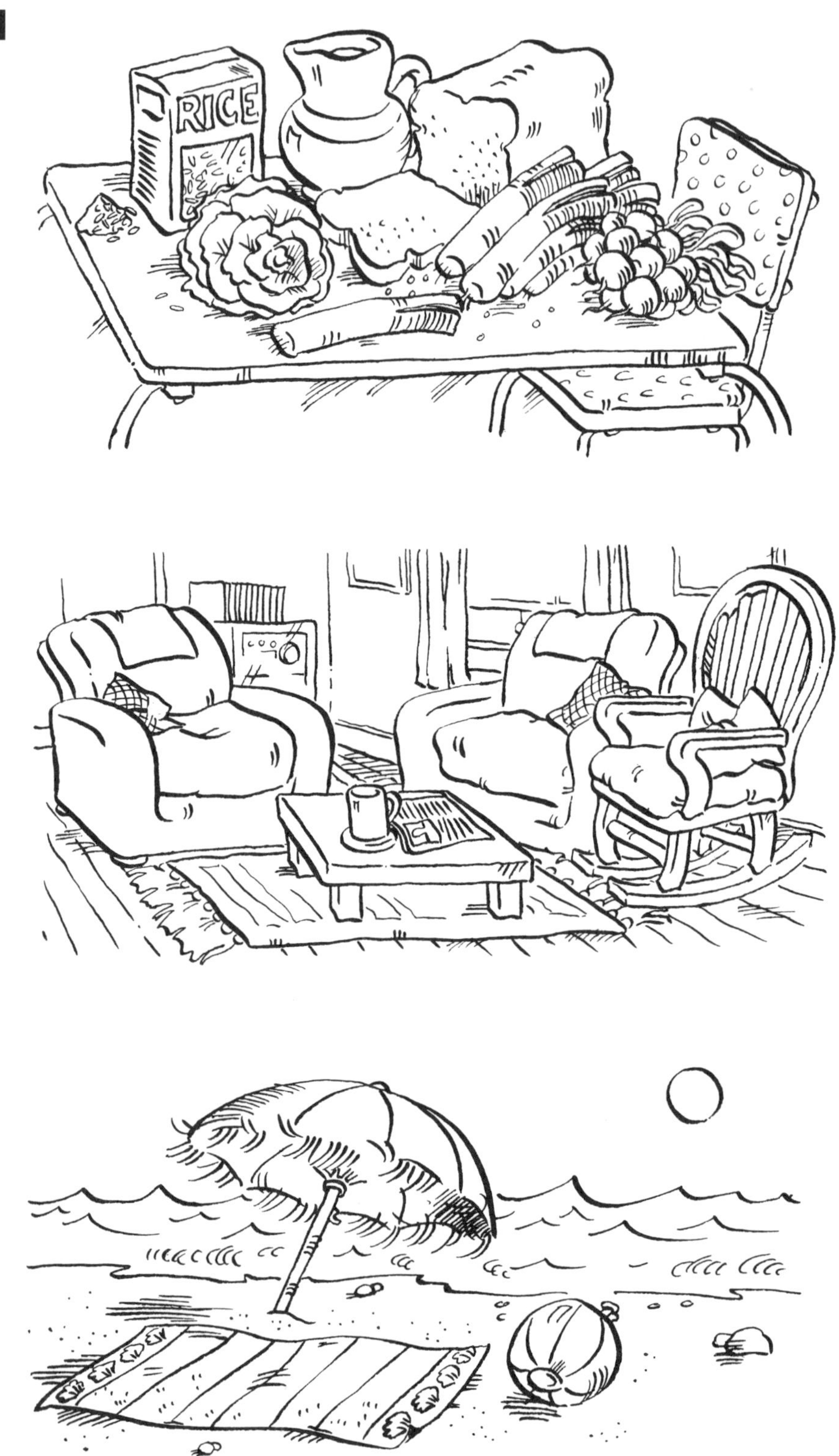
RICE

8
Focus on receptive skills

The activities in this chapter aim to practise both listening and reading skills. As with other chapters, the main aim is to provide motivating activities which will encourage students to listen and read outside class. The benefits of these activities are:

- They increase students' exposure to language in a variety of contexts.
- Students will recognize class-taught language outside class, which will make the classroom language seem more relevant.
- Students will practise the two skills at their own pace.

As David Nunan says in *Language Teaching Methodology*, 'There is constant interplay between listening, speaking, reading and writing, and it is clear that in a lesson which is ostensibly labeled "reading", opportunities exist for learners to develop their other language skills as well.' Benefits include vocabulary enrichment, pronunciation work (in a listening lesson), and reinforcement of grammatical structures, because students can see them in context.

Ensuring that students do read and listen is the main difficulty for a teacher. Often I have set work to be read in preparation for a lesson, only to find that the students haven't read it. Why don't they read? Is it because they can't see the value of it? Do they have a lot of time constraints? Don't they find the required materials stimulating? Each of these questions needs to be addressed in order to succeed in setting useful reading and listening activities.

In this chapter, I suggest resources that I think students will have access to and will find interesting. Most students go to the cinema in their free time, so a movie activity like 8.1, 'Let's go to the movies', is likely to be motivating. Exploiting students' enjoyment of the Internet in homework tasks is also useful. Television and radio are obvious resources to be tapped, and are universal in their appeal. Try to set tasks that allow the students to use activities they already do, such as surfing the Internet, for a linguistic purpose.

Activities 8.2, 'Notes from the news', and 8.3, 'Listening to advertisements', depend on the students having access to English-speaking television or radio, such as CNN, MTV, or the BBC World Service. I have found it helpful to write the details of such channels on poster card and display them in class for students. If the students find other television or radio stations or other resources, they should be encouraged to add them to your list.

8.1 Let's go to the movies

Level Intermediate and above

Time IN CLASS 10–15 minutes
HOMEWORK The length of the movie plus 10–15 minutes

Aims To use students' enjoyment of the cinema to promote language learning.

Preparation

Watch a current English-speaking movie. Note down as much information about the film as you can, such as where it is set, the characters' and actors' names, events, the ending, and so on. Prepare a list of facts about the movie for students, but make sure that some are false. For example, the movie was set in Mexico (true). The leading character's name was Herbert (false—it was John), and so on. Photocopy your list for each student.

Procedure

1. Set the students the homework task of watching the movie. Provide them with your list of facts about it.
2. Tell them that some of the facts are false, and what they must do is watch the movie and note down which facts are true and which are false.
3. When the students are back in class, ask them to compare their answers with their partner. Discuss the answers with the class.

Comments

Students may watch a movie with subtitles, but encourage them to listen and watch as much as possible without reading the subtitles.

Variation

Give the students this worksheet to answer after they have watched the movie.

Questionnaire

1. Where was the movie set?
2. What time was the story set in?
3. What were the main characters' names?
4. What type of movie genre is it—for example, horror, romance?
5. What are the main actors' names?
6. Describe the main plot.

The students can report the answers to the rest of the class once they have seen the movie. The answers must be written in English.

Follow-up

The students can write a review of the movie for homework.

8.2 Notes from the news

Level Intermediate and above

Time IN CLASS 5–10 minutes
HOMEWORK 20–30 minutes

Aims **To encourage students to listen for both general and detailed information using an authentic listening source. This will improve not only their listening skills but also their general ability to comprehend spoken English.**

Preparation

Find out when the news is broadcast in English on the radio, for example, on the BBC World Service. Listen to current news stories.

Procedure

1. At the end of a class, give the students information about English-speaking news on radio, including times and frequency.
2. Set them the homework task of listening to a news broadcast and taking notes about the news. Encourage them to note as much as they can and not to be deterred if it is difficult at first for them to understand.
3. In the following lesson, ask the students, in pairs, to tell each other what they heard.

Variation

If students all have access to the Internet, choose a news site such as www.bbc.co.uk or www.cnn.com.

Visit the sites to see what is available. Explain to the students how to find the site you choose and ask them to look at the news broadcast on the Internet. If the students have speakers on their computers, they will be able to use this as a listening resource also. In class, check what the students listened to and how well they understood it. Correct their mistakes.

8.3 Listening to advertisements

Level Upper-intermediate and above

Time IN CLASS 10 minutes
HOMEWORK 20 minutes per session

Aims To practise listening for detailed information using an authentic source.

Preparation

Find one or more English-speaking television channels or radio stations with advertisements, to which the students can gain access. MTV and CNN are good sources for this.

Procedure

1 Ask the students to listen to or watch an advertisement in English on the radio or television. They should find out what is being advertised, what the product or service offers, and who would benefit from it. Advertisements are usually repeated, therefore the students can catch their selected advert again, or they could tape it and play it repeatedly in order to answer the questions fully.

2 In class, organize the students into pairs and tell them to explain the advertisement that they listened to.

Comments

1 Advertisements are motivating because they are short, and very often use up-to-date language.

2 A teenage learner group I taught, who were addicted to MTV, followed up this activity by acting out an advertisement for a soft drink. It was fun and also showed how much they had understood.

8.4 A scene from your favourite programme

Level Intermediate and above

Time IN CLASS 30 minutes
HOMEWORK 40 minutes +

Aims To encourage students to listen for both detail and general information. Also to consider pronunciation, especially intonation, and how it is modified for the feelings in a scene.

Preparation

Find out about television programmes in English. Note down times and days.

Procedure

1 Ask your students in class what they regularly watch on television. Then ask them what they watch in English. If they don't watch anything, set them the task of finding a television programme that they could watch. Give them the information regarding times and programmes you have gathered, and ask them to do research at home.

2 When a programme has been selected, set these questions:
1 What is the programme about?
2 Who are the main characters?
3 What happened when you watched?
4 Where is it filmed?
5 Why do you like it?

Ask the students to watch the programme at home and answer the questions.

3 Ask the students to present their answers to the rest of the class.

Variation 1

1 Ask all the students or groups of students to watch a particular episode of a programme very closely. The students should note down:
- the characters
- what happened in one scene
- the dialogue (roughly) of that scene.

2 Back in class, the students should re-enact chosen scenes using their notes. They should assign roles and give a brief synopsis of what happened and what the programme is about. This activity practises writing skills along with listening skills.

Variation 2

If the students cannot find a suitable programme in English, they can use a programme in their own language, but tell them to translate the score and do the task in English.

8.5 Transcribe a song

Level Upper-intermediate and above

Time IN CLASS 20 minutes
HOMEWORK 60 minutes +

Aims To exploit material which students already listen to; to practise the ability to listen for detail.

Preparation

Ask the students to tell you what kind of music they listen to and how many British, North American, or English-speaking singers they listen to. Ask them whether they have any of their music on CDs, MDs, or cassettes. The students will need access to recordings for the task.

Procedure

1 At the end of a lesson, tell the students that you would like them to choose a song in English and transcribe the lyrics for homework. They should bring the transcribed lyrics to show you and the other students.

2 In order to check the lyrics, either borrow the music or look up the lyrics on the Internet (see Appendix for Internet resources).

Variation

Ask the students to choose a song in their own language to translate into English. I did this in Poland and needed the school administrative assistants to help correct the work (I bought them flowers before asking them to help!). Stipulate the type of music you'd like, such as traditional or popular, and check with native speakers as to its appropriateness.

Follow-up

Use the songs in class for varying listening tasks. Each time you do, tell the class which student transcribed the song.

8.6 Song lyrics

Level Intermediate and above

Time IN CLASS 15–20 minutes
HOMEWORK 30–50 minutes

Aims **To encourage students to listen to songs in English; they will also practise their writing skills as they will answer in complete sentences.**

Materials

A song on tape or disc, and the means to play it.

Preparation

Copy out the lyrics of a song which you can play in class.

Procedure

1 Give the students the lyrics, and dictate questions to be answered. Ask the students for homework to read the lyrics and answer the questions.

Examples
1 What type of music do you think it is?
2 Who is singing?
3 What is he or she singing about?
4 Is it happy or sad?
5 Where is the song set?
6 Has something just happened?
7 Is something about to happen?

2 When the students are back in class, ask them to compare their answers with each other. Collect their answers and play the song to them. You may want to design a particular lesson around the song, or you can simply ask the students to discuss their answers and whether they liked the song.

8.7 Famous person

Level Intermediate and above

Time IN CLASS 20 minutes (optional)
HOMEWORK 50–80 minutes

Aims To encourage reading for detailed information about an interesting theme. To provide students with exposure to authentic materials.

Preparation

Choose a suitable famous person and collect interesting information about him or her. This could be someone from your students' locality, or an international movie or pop star. Try to find some unusual information which is not commonly known about this person.

Procedure

1 At the end of a class, tell the students about your chosen person.

2 Ask the students for homework to find out interesting facts about a famous person. Guide the students as to where to find the information, for example, on the Internet, in library books, magazines, etc. If the students use the Internet, it is a good idea to list useful sites for them (see Appendix).

3 Back in class, ask the students to give presentations about their chosen person; these presentations could be filmed or taped if you have a small group. If you have a large group, ask the students to display their work in class.

Variation 1

Younger learners could make a collage in class of their work.

Variation 2

Business people can research successful businessmen and -women they admire.

Variation 3

If you think the students need clearer guidelines, give them the worksheet on the next page.

Famous person	
Name:	______
Date of birth (and death):	______
Country of origin:	______
Important achievements:	______
	______
	______
	______
Facts that are not well known:	______
	______
	______
	______

8.8 Dictate a puzzle

Level **Intermediate and above**

Time **IN CLASS** **20–30 minutes**
HOMEWORK **60 minutes + (less for some students)**

Aims **In class: listening for detailed information. At home: reading.**

Preparation

Choose one or more brainteaser-type puzzles (see the examples below) for your class.

Procedure

1. In the last 20–30 minutes of a class, tell the students that you are going to set them puzzles to which they need to find the solution before the next lesson.
2. Dictate the puzzles.

Examples A man sits in a restaurant. He orders water. The waiter comes back with a gun. He fires the gun. The man says thank you. Why did this happen?

Answer: The man ordered water because he had hiccoughs. The waiter fired the gun and scared him, which stopped the hiccoughs. That is why the man said thank you.

There's a blind man [you may want to say 'visually impaired' if you prefer politically correct language] in a prison with one window. The sun shines through the window. He has two balls, one white and one black. How can he tell which is which?

Answer: The black one absorbs the sunlight because it is black and so it gets hotter than the white one.

3 In the following class, ask the students for their answers and if necessary tell them the correct answers.

Follow-up

If they enjoyed this task, ask them to think of similar puzzles in their own language and for homework to translate them. Collect them during the following lesson and correct the English. Repeat the homework activity using the students' puzzles.

A teenage learner group that I taught kept bringing such puzzles to class and I made a collage of them. Visitors to the class enjoyed reading and puzzling over them.

Comments

These puzzles can be great fun. They provide a clear reason for reading and listening—to work out the solution.

8.9 Jigsaw

Level Intermediate and above

Time IN CLASS 10 minutes
HOMEWORK 45 minutes

Aims To encourage students to read for general and detailed information, and to read authentic materials as much as possible.

Preparation

Find a suitable text (like the example on the next page) for your students from a magazine, newspaper, or downloaded from the Internet. Cut the text up into large pieces so each student can have a section of it.

Procedure

1 Give the students the pieces of text. Don't tell them where the text has come from, but dictate the title to the whole group.

2 Set the students the questions on page 131 (or similar) for homework.

Mystery as postcard arrives 80 years late

A POSTCARD sent by a British soldier serving in France in the First World War has been delivered after almost 80 years. Alan Rawsthorne, 49, said he was amazed when the card arrived through the letterbox at his home on Cedar Road in Stockport, Greater Manchester.

Dated July 24 1918 and addressed to a Miss Hunt, it is signed 'George' and pictures a French chateau. It reads 'Met Jack yesterday. Tell him when you write. I haven't seen this (the chateau) but it's somewhere near where we are.

'I discovered a YMCA last night. A one centime can be a cup of tea and biscuits at night. The younger lads are having a game at football.

'Glorious day nice cool breeze. Not moved so far. George'.

There is a French postal mark dated July 26 1918 and a stamp from the censor, who apparently obliterated the name of the chateau on the front but left a printed name—M Emmanuel de Palmaert—intact.

Mr Rawsthorne, a landscape gardener, said yesterday: 'It's unbelieveable and very intriguing.'

Sister

'We've done some investigating and found that there was a Miss Kate Hunt living here in 1918 and a George Hunt in 1920 so we think he might have been writing to his sister while he was away.

'I'd love to know why it took so long to get here because I don't believe it is a hoax. Who would go to all that trouble?

'We'd love to make contact with any descendants of the Hunts to give them the card and find out more about them.'

A Royal Mail spokeswoman said: 'It is a mystery but we have carried out extensive checks and there is no evidence to show that the card has been delayed in the postal system.

'Normally procedure would be to send out a covering letter to apologise if an item has been delayed.

'If it had been popped back into the system then it would have a second postal mark or a surcharge stamp.'

Shropshire Star 7 March 1998

1 What is the text about?
2 Which type of magazine or book is it from—science fiction, sports magazine, etc?
3 Which part of the text is this, the beginning, the middle, or the end?
4 Add one more sentence to the beginning or the end of your text.

3 During the next class, students should present their answers and then physically piece together the text, by standing in sequential order.

Variation

Give the students pieces of different texts rather than just one text.

8.10 Find authentic material

Level Intermediate and above

Time IN CLASS 15–30 minutes
HOMEWORK 40–50 minutes

Aims To encourage students to find out about each other and to find a text they would like to read.

Procedure

1 Brainstorm the types of topics that the students enjoy reading about and the types of authentic materials they have already read in class. If necessary, show examples of texts. The one on the next page contains good examples of the present perfect, idioms, and conditional language.
2 Explain to the students that their homework task is to find a reading text for the whole group. The text must be appealing, motivating, and appropriate for the class.
3 In the following lesson, the students should present their materials to the group explaining why they chose that particular text. For example, the vocabulary was interesting with a lot of useful, new words.
4 Display the materials in the classroom so that the students can read them; use the materials in class or set the materials as homework for other students to read.

8.10

Example

Mary, 88, shows the way behind the bar

A TELFORD octogenarian showed she still has what it takes by pulling the perfect pint in a pub she worked at more than 60 years ago. Mary Bloomfield, 88, from Madeley, put the current bar staff to shame when she dropped in at the Chance Hotel where she worked as a teenager. The visit to the bar in Coventry was arranged by the ExtraCare Charitable Trust, which owns the Lady Forester Nursing Home.

Mary moved to the Much Wenlock home at Christmas and often talked about wanting to go back to see how the bar had changed since she moved back to Madeley. The trust decided to make her dreams come true.

After having lunch in the restaurant where Mary once served dinners to customers, the sprightly pensioner was taken on a tour of the building, telling staff what changes there had been over the years. She kept everyone entertained with stories of the things she used to get up to and about some of the characters she used to serve.

Before she left Mary asked if she could go behind the bar for one last time and showed the staff that she still had plenty of pulling power.

When asked how she felt about being behind the bar again, Mary said: 'My brain just switches my age off. I feel like a 16-year-old again.'

Source: *Shropshire Star* 29 April 2002

Variation

Organize the students into pairs and have them ask each other questions like the ones below to find out what type of reading material each person likes. As homework, based on the discussions in class, ask each student to find a text for his or her partner.

1. When you have free time, what do you like to read?
2. When you read a newspaper, what do you like to read first: sports, news, entertainment pages?
3. If you take books with you on vacation, what types do you take?
4. Do you play a lot of sports, or use the Internet a lot? What are your hobbies?

8.11 Find the site

Level Intermediate and above

Time IN CLASS 10–15 minutes
HOMEWORK 45 minutes

Aims This involves an activity that students probably already do in their free time—surfing the Internet. It encourages students to surf in English rather than their first language.

Preparation

Photocopy the questionnaire below for each student in class.

1. What do you like to watch on television?
2. What type of books do you read?
3. What do you like to do in your free time?
4. What interests you? Are you interested in politics, sports, cooking, other countries and cultures, science, animals, history, economics, business, current events?
5. When you surf the Internet, where do you go?
6. What favourites have you marked?

Procedure

1. Hand out the questionnaire and ask the students to mingle and find out each other's interests by asking each other the questions.
2. Set the students the homework task of finding a website, in English, that they think one or two of their classmates would be interested in.
3. Back in class, the students should give each other the addresses of sites that they think would be appropriate, explaining why they chose them.

8.12 English in my town

Level Pre-intermediate and above

Time IN CLASS 10–15 minutes
HOMEWORK 45–60 minutes

Aims To heighten the students' awareness of English in their own area.

Preparation

Find a street map of your town or city, and mark places where the English language can be found on billboards, store signs, road signs, etc. Copy your map for each student.

Procedure

1 Give the students the map and ask them for homework to find the places marked and note down the exact wording of English they see there.

2 When the students are in class, they should tell the rest of the group what they have read.

Follow-up

Ask the students to look for other places in which there are signs in English, and to mark them on a large town map which can be displayed in class. A variety of reading tasks based on English outside class can be designed.

Examples

1 In Rose Street, how does the sign tell us to think?
Answer: Think differently (a computer advertisement)

2 What is being shown at the cinema? What type of movie is it?
Answer: The *Wedding Planner*, a love story

3 What should you do when driving at the corner of Polawski Street?
Answer: Stop!

4 Where can you buy English and American magazines?
Answer: The Grand Hotel

5 Where can you get tourist information?
Answer: The corner of Bayard and Baxter Street

8.13 Vocabulary to teach my class

Level Pre-intermediate and above

Time IN CLASS 20–25 minutes
HOMEWORK 40 minutes +

Aims To encourage students to be independent learners and to find out what is useful for them. It can help you decide what to teach in your lessons.

Preparation

Copy the worksheet on the next page for each student.

Lexical item	Meaning	Part of speech	Example sentence
1			
2			
3			
4			
5			

Procedure

1. Ask the students which magazines or papers they read in English. Ask them to read a news article at home from the Internet, a news magazine such as *Newsweek*, or a newspaper. If students cannot get hold of a text, provide them with magazines.
2. Set the students the task of finding five lexical items from their chosen text that they think their classmates should know. Give them copies of the worksheet to complete.
3. Explain that they should write the new lexical items down and research their meanings, using a dictionary and guessing the meaning from the context of the article.
4. Back in class, the students should describe the text they read and the new lexical items.

Variation 1

The students could write their words down on cards and place them in the English bag, if you have completed Activity 3.4, 'English bag', and kept your bag in class.

Variation 2

Students could be asked to look for lexical items for a particular person in class, for example: *Juan is a computer analyst. Find five words that you think would be useful for him.*

8.14 Write your own comprehension questions

Level Elementary and above (depending on the texts you choose)

Time IN CLASS 20 minutes
HOMEWORK 45–55 minutes

Aims To provide practice in writing questions in English as well as reading for detailed information.

Preparation

Find an example of comprehension questions to show the students. Find and copy different reading texts for each student.

Procedure

1. Show the students an example of comprehension questions, possibly from their course books, and tell them they are going to write similar questions for a text.
2. Hand out a text to each student and ask them for homework to write ten questions.
3. During the following lesson, collect the texts and questions, correct them and then redistribute the questions and texts to different students. Ask the students to complete these questions for homework.

Variation

Lower-level students could be asked to write true/false questions rather than open questions. They can therefore write in the form of statements.

8.15 Read the article!

Level Intermediate and above

Time IN CLASS 30–40 minutes
HOMEWORK 30–40 minutes

Aims To encourage students to read for a specific purpose, i.e. to develop an argument for a debate in class.

Preparation

Chose an article which is polemical and provokes the reader; the students should have strong opinions after they have read it.

Procedure

1. Ask the students to read the article at home.
2. Tell the students they will be asked their opinion about the topic of the article in class, so they should make notes on arguments for and against, and any questions they think of as they are reading. Next, they should consider how they will present their opinions to the class.
3. In class, hold a debate.

Follow-up

Schedule time at the beginning or end of lessons in which students can discuss articles they have read recently, and which they hold strong opinions about. Ask them to write questions that they would like to ask the author of the article.

Comments

Students have time to prepare their opinions so they should be more fluent when using English in class.

8.16 Give out the headlines

Level Pre-intermediate and above

Time IN CLASS 10–15 minutes
HOMEWORK 30–45 minutes

Aims To encourage students to read the news in English.

Preparation

Cut out or note down the headlines from the day's news.

Procedure

1. At the end of a lesson, show or dictate headlines from the news to the students.
2. Ask them to find out what these stories are about for homework. They can research the news on the Internet or read newspapers in their own language and translate.
3. In the next lesson, ask them, in pairs, to tell each other what the stories were about. Monitor this and at the end of the activity make sure that the students have found the correct stories.

Comments

I found this very successful with business English groups, who had access to the Internet and read the news anyway.

Follow-up

If possible, encourage the students to find headlines in English outside class, and then repeat the activity. The students should dictate or show the headlines and other students should research the items for homework.

8.17 Cultural awareness

Level Upper-intermediate and above

Time IN CLASS 20 minutes
HOMEWORK 30–40 minutes

Aims To encourage students to find out about other cultures whilst practising their ability to read in detail.

Procedure

1. Tell the students that their homework task is to find an article about an English-speaking country, for example, England or America. The article can be from any source, including the Internet and CNN, and about any topic, for example, crime, education, fashion, etc. When the students are reading the article they should compare the culture they are reading about to their own, and write down the differences and their opinions in note form below or by annotating the text.
2. In class, ask the students to summarize their articles and present their research about cultural differences to the group. They can swap notes or annotated versions so they can see exactly which points in the text were of interest.

Follow-up

Name a country and ask students to find out certain information about it to bring into class and present. Each student should find a different piece of information. The Internet could be used as a source.

Examples

1. Find a historical fact from the 19th century.
2. Find a recipe.
3. Find a beauty spot.
4. Name an export product.
5. Name a famous person.
6. Name a famous book, poem, or song about the country.
7. Name a famous entertainer.
8. Find a strange fact.
9. Describe a political event.
10. Name some typical foods and drinks.

Comments

Younger learners may want to create a wall collage with this information.

8.18 Gossip

Level Intermediate and above

Time IN CLASS 20 minutes
HOMEWORK 45–50 minutes

Aims To motivate students to read fun things in English.

Preparation

Find out information in the news about famous people your students will know, and then add some false rumours—for example, that Madonna is having another baby, the leader of the country is going to resign, and so on. You should make a list of up to ten pieces of information and misinformation.

Procedure

1 Ask the students to think about news they have heard about famous people in their country or internationally recently, for example, a politician may be getting married, a famous actor may be making a new movie, etc.

2 Dictate your 'headlines' to the students. For homework, they have to research your information and decide whether the stories are true or false. Instruct the students that they must find a source that has been written in English, for example, on the Internet, in a magazine, etc. To ensure that the students read in English, they must quote their source.

3 During the next lesson, the students should be asked which of the stories are true and which are false.

Variation

Use true and false historical facts as the information the students have to research.

1 In class, ask the students to think of some important historical dates. These dates may be connected to their own country or be internationally recognized, for example, the dates of the Second World War, the date President John F. Kennedy was assassinated, etc.

2 Dictate some true and false dates from history to the students. Ask them to research these from sources written in English, to discover whether the information is true or false.

Examples
1 The First World War began in 1910.
2 The *Titanic* sank in 1890.
3 The Second World War began in 1939.

8.19 Baking

Level Elementary and above

Time IN CLASS 10–15 minutes
HOMEWORK 45–60 minutes

Aims To provide students with a reason for reading, especially those students who are interested in cooking.

Preparation

Photocopy the recipe opposite (it is for scones) for everyone in the class.

Procedure

1 After you have taught a lesson on food and recipe instructions, give each student in the class the recipe below.

Ingredients

225g self-raising flour
50g butter
25g caster sugar
50g currants or sultanas
1 medium egg, beaten with enough milk to make 150ml
Pinch of salt

Instructions

Rub the flour and butter together in a bowl until it looks like breadcrumbs. Stir in the sugar, salt and currants or sultanas. Add the egg mixture to make a soft dough. Put the dough on to a floured board, and knead it lightly. Roll out the dough and cut into circles. Bake these at 400°F (200°C) in a preheated oven for about 18 minutes. Allow to cool.

2 Ask them to go home and make the dish in the recipe, following the instructions. Don't give the students any clues as to what the recipe makes; tell them that it is simple and delicious, and they can bring the results to the next class.

Comments

This activity is especially useful for students who enjoy doing, rather than simply sitting down and studying.

Variation

If you prefer not to ask the students to make food, ask them to make something else, for example, a 'snap dragon'. Make one yourself—you may have done this as a child.

1 Give each student in the class a square sheet of paper. Give them the instructions below and ask them to use the paper and the instructions to make something. Do not tell them what it makes. Ask them to bring the result to the next class.

> **Instructions**
>
> Fold the piece of paper in half, open it, and then fold it in half again on the opposite side. Open the paper again. Take each corner and fold it into the middle of the square. Turn the folded square over and fold the corners into the middle again. Fold the new shape in half, open it and then fold it in half on the opposite side. Open it again. Put your index fingers and thumbs under the four flaps at the lower corners and manipulate the shape.

2 In the following lesson, see what the students have made and show them what it should look like. Very often the students know what this is and can make it easily. As a follow-up activity you can play word games with these toys, by writing under the flaps.

Appendix

Useful websites for English learners

The number of websites dedicated to English language students is phenomenal, and possibly intimidating. Try the ones listed below, and bookmark the ones you find useful. These are favourites that I have found invaluable in providing resources for both myself and my students. They were accessible at the time of going to press. A lot of research can also be done at www.google.com or www. yahoo.com

Your students may be well versed in surfing on the net, and therefore need only prompts as to where they should look. If some students don't have access to the Internet, try to pair them with others in the class who do. Find out about public Internet access in your locality—is there a library that students can go to, or a cyber café? You could make this a homework activity in itself—researching the local resources. Make sure you ask the students to research specifics, i.e. times when the library is open, how much it costs to use the Internet, etc.

Vocabulary websites

www.fun-with-words.com
This is useful for ideas to do with vocabulary, including oxymorons, palindromes, etc.

www.eslcafe.com
This website has a comprehensive list of phrasal verbs and idioms, as well as forums for English language learners. This may be useful for students who would like to contact other learners.

www.eslsite.com
This has a variety of worksheets that students could print out and use, along with classroom resources for teachers.

General interest websites

www.bbc.co.uk
The BBC website offers news and general interest articles. Teachers may want to monitor this site for useful articles students could read. The radio section includes recordings of programmes that can be listened to online.

www.cnn.com
CNN's website provides students with exposure to American English. Students could read a BBC news story and a CNN news story on the same topic and compare the reporting styles and language used.
www.historychannel.com This American website offers interesting historical information, which can be useful for setting up research projects.

www.worldalmanacforkids.com
This is a useful resource for younger learners when researching factual information.

www.people.com
Students can find out about famous people at this site.

www.lyrics.com
This site contains song lyrics.

www.resourcehelp.com
A directory of internet resources on many topics

Teacher resources

www.oup.com/elt/global/teachersclub/

www.teflfarm.com

www.tefl.net

www.tefl.com

Bibliography

Bobbitt, S. (ed.). 1998. *Helping Your Students with Homework: A Guide for Teachers*. Washington, D.C.: Office of Educational Research and Improvement, U.S. Department of Education. Available online at http://www.ed.gov/pubs/HelpingStudents/

Bowen, T. and **J. Marks.** 1994. *Inside Teaching.* Oxford: Heinemann.

Brumfit, C. J. and **K. Johnson.** 1994. *The Communicative Approach to Language Teaching.* Oxford: Oxford University Press.

Cooper, H. 2001. *The Battle over Homework: Common Ground for Administrators, Teachers, and Parents* (2nd edn.). Thousand Oaks, CA: Corwin Press.

Chaika, G. 2000. 'Help! Homework is wrecking my home life.' *Education World* 8/8/2000. http://www.educationworld.com/a_admin/admin182.shtml

Doff, A. 1984. *Teach English*. Cambridge: Cambridge University Press.

Gilbert, J. 'Think Tank.' *ELT News* December 2001. http://www.eltnews.com/features/thinktank/007_2.shtml#judy

Graham, C. 1978. *Jazz Chants.* Oxford: Oxford University Press.

Hedge, T. 1988. *Writing.* Oxford: Oxford University Press.

North, S. and **H. Pillay.** 2002. 'Homework: re-examining the routine.' *ELT Journal* 56/2: 137–45.

Nunan, D. 1991. *Language Teaching Methodology.* Englewood Cliffs: Prentice Hall International.

Richards, J. C. 1997. *The Context of Language Teaching*. Cambridge: Cambridge University Press

Rubin, J. and **I. Thompson.** 1994. *How to be a More Successful Language Learner.* Boston: Heinle and Heinle.

Soars, J. and **L. Soars.** 1987. *Headway Intermediate.* Oxford: Oxford University Press.

Stern, H. H. 1991. *Fundamental Concepts of Language Teaching*. Oxford: Oxford University Press.

Stevick, E. W. 1998. *Working with Teaching Methods.* Heinle and Heinle.

Ur, P. 1996. *A Course in Language Teaching.* Cambridge: Cambridge University Press.

Watcyn-Jones, P. 1978. *Act English*. London: Penguin (out of print).

Widdowson, H. G. 1990. *Aspects of Language Teaching*. Oxford: Oxford University Press.

Woodward, T. 1991. *Models and Metaphors in Language Teacher Training*. Cambridge: Cambridge University Press.

Wright, J. 1998. *Dictionaries*. Oxford: Oxford University Press.

Zentall, S. S. and **S. Goldstein.** 1999. *Seven Steps to Homework Success: A Family Guide for Solving Common Homework Problems*. Plantation, Florida: Specialty Press, Inc.

Index

In the general index references are to page numbers; in the *Topics* and *Language and Skills* indexes references are to activity numbers. Some terms, such as 'feedback', may appear in more than one index

General Index

aims of homework 6
business students 87, 127, 137
curriculum focus 13
dictionary skills 14–15
examples of language in use 37
feedback 15
fun themes 8
grammar 71
learning preferences 9–10
memory 14, 37–8
monitoring homework 15
news 37
questionnaires 10, 13
re-evaluating homework 6–8
relevance 8–9
time commitment 11
trips 87
usage 36
websites 142–3
writing 56–7

Topics

advertisements **3.8, 8.3**
art gallery **6.11**
authentic tasks **6.2, 6.13**
baking **8.19**
bank **6.13**
body idioms **3.11**
cartoons **2.3**
chants **5.14, 7.3**
cinema **2.3, 8.1**
colour coding **5.5**
comments **1.3**
context **5.8**
correction **1.2**
crosswords **3.15**
cue cards **6.4**
cultural awareness **3.10, 6.16, 8.17**
diaries **4.1**
differences **5.12, 7.2**
email **1.6**
English bag (storing vocabulary) **3.4**
envelopes, homework in **1.4**
excuses **2.7**
famous people **4.1, 8.7**
favorite tasks **2.2**
feedback **2.1**
gap-fill worksheets **5.2**
gossip **8.18**
graffiti **4.12**
grocery store **6.13**
headlines **8.16**
homework books **1.1**
internet **8.11**
jigsaw **8.9**
journals **6.8**
mission impossible (variety) **1.5**
motivation **1.4, 2.2, 2.4, 8.18**
movies **2.3, 8.1**
museum visit **6.12**
news **3.3, 4.6, 8.2, 8.16**
pharmacy **6.1**
photographs **4.9**
pictures **6.10, 7.11**
post office **6.13**
professions **4.1**
pules **8.8**
questionnaires **2.1**
quizzes **5.13**
recipes **8.19**
role play **6.15**
scrapbooks **4.8**
setting up homework **2.1**
songs **2.2, 8.5, 8.6**
tape recordings **6.8, 6.9**
telephone **6.5, 6.6**
television **5.7, 8.4**
tongue twisters **7.3**
unusual facts **4.6**
variety **1.5**
zoo visit **6.14**

Language and skills

antonyms **3.4**
authentic materials, using **3.8, 8.3, 8.7, 8.9, 8.10**
beginner confidence, developing **6.3**
collocations **3.7**
connected speech **7.5**
conversation **6.1**
correcting errors **1.2, 5.10**
debating skills **8.15**
describing pictures **6.10**
designing homework tasks **2.3**
dictionary work **2.3, 7.8, 7.9**
doubles **3.12**
examples in use **3.2, 5.1, 5.6, 8.12**
expressions **3.10**
false friends **3.9**
first language **5.12**
fun dialogues **1.3**
functional language **6.2, 6.13**
idioms **3.1, 3.9, 3.11**
information sharing (personal) **5.3**
integrated skills **4.8**
intonation **7.10, 8.4**
learning independently **8.13**
letter writing **2.5, 4.2–4**
lexical items *see* vocabulary
lexical sets **6.3**
memorizing language **5.8, 5.9, 6.4, 6.7**
metaphors **2.2**
minimal pairs **7.7**
note-taking **4.6**
oral presentations **6.10, 6.12, 8.7**
oxymorons **3.13**
palindromes **3.14**
past continuous **6.1**
past participles **5.4**
past simple **5.4, 6.1**
phonemes **2.2, 3.4, 7.4, 7.5**
present participles **5.4**
present simple **5.9**
presenting information **4.7**
questions **4.11, 5.11, 6.1, 6.6, 6.7, 8.14**
researching information **4.7**
rhymes **5.4, 5.14, 7.3**
rhythm **5.14**
schwa **7.1**
simple past **5.4, 6.1**
simple present **5.9**
skills work **2.4**
sounds **7.2, 7.3, 7.6, 7.11**
spelling **3.5, 3.6, 3.14**
story telling **4.5, 4.10, 4.12**
stress **7.8, 7.9**
teaching others **2.6**
tenses **5.5, 5.13**
transcribing sentences into phonemic script **7.5**
transcribing a song **8.5**
usage **3.1, 5.6**
verb cue cards **6.4**
vocabulary **3.4, 3.5, 8.13**
word box **3.6**
word review **3.5**